# THE UNFORGETTABLE PAST

## A STORY OF PAIN, DILEMMA, MYSTERY, AND AN UNUSUAL ROMANCE

### BY
### NIPLA HASIJA

ALL RIGHTS RESERVED
MANUFACTURED IN TORONTO
ISBN: 0-9696767-1-9

Canadian Cataloguing in Publication Data

Hasija, Nipla, 1918–
    The unforgettable past

I. Title.

PS8565.A722U5 1996    C813 ' .54    C96–931623–2
PR9199 .3 .H3617U5 1996

NEW AGE ( N.A.G.E. ) PUBLISHING
TORONTO, ONTARIO

**DEDICATION**

**AT THE LOTUS FEET
OF
THE LORD**

# THE AUTHOR

Mrs. Nipla Hasija was born in the year 1918, in Lahore.

She is the mother of seven children. Four of her sons have served and are serving as Army Colonels in the Indian Army.

She holds a masters' degree in English and is also a doctor in homeopathy.

Mrs. Hasija is a member of the Writer's Union of Canada For the last several years.

She has travelled widely and has published several works including poetry, short stories, religious books and fiction both in the English and the Hindi language, in India and America.

At the age of 73 she received a diploma from the International Correspondence School of Montreal, for Journalism and Short story writing.

Throughout her career as Principal of Higher Secondary and Junior Teacher's Training Schools, she had introduced several new experiments successfully in child education. She now is trying to put together all these innovations to improve the child education system, in Canada, and has been working on it for the past couple of years. She has almost completed an educational theme for the Kindergarten Class, and hopes to get it published very soon.

NEW AGE (N.A.G.E.)PUBLISHING

FORWARD

THE UNFORGETTABLE PAST

BY

NIPLA HASIJA

It is a poignant, emotionally evocative story of a beautiful widow in love with a handsome, virile doctor recently returned from England.

The heroine is in constant pain and misery, since she has no choice but to conceal her feelings from him  not only because she found out that he was in love with a young and beautiful person, daughter of the chief Minister of a state, but also due to a strange  quirk  of fate;   not being sure of....................?

'WHO FATHERED BOTH HER CHILDREN'

From its spirited beginning to its fast paced exposition and heart rending conclusion, Nipla Hasija has created a reading expcrience.  She offers adventure, romance and many vivid three dimensional characters.

Mention must also be made of the universality of the plot. Despite its foreign background,   the reader   will identify with Sonia, her children, with Knawal and his mother.   Its a book of masterful plot, imaginative complications and realistic characters.  It will please all who read it.  The ordeal of body and mind, the quest for inner peace and outer contentment--is the theme of the story.

Once you have read the first page you'll be unable to put it down.

In addition those who are unacquainted with India will be awarded a taste of the land...its food, customs, marital practices, and tradition of the two hundred million white collar, highly educated people of India, living in cities.

Nipla Hasija engrosses the reader's imagination, and interests, with her writing skills.

Editor

# CHAPTER 1

The telephone beside the bed began to ring. Sonia picked up the receiver. "Hello, Sonia speaking."

"May I speak to Tara?" asked Radha from the other end.

"Mother is not home. Can I take a message?"

"She wanted me to call her when I went for Sai Baba's* bhajans.*

"At what time the bhajan starts?"

"Six in the evening."

"Mother won't be in till six thirty in the evening. May I join you for the bhajans?"

"Sure. I'll pick you up at five thirty."

On the way Radha said, "I'm very happy these days.

* A saint.　　　* hymn

A couple of days back my son returned from England after fourteen years."

"What was he doing in England?"

"He's a heart specialist. He was working at the St. Paul's hospital in London."

My husband too worked in that hospital. What's his name?" "Kanwal Khanna."

"What a small world:" Sonia exclaimed.

"Do you know him?"

"I haven't met him personally; but I know he was a fast friend of\ my husband."Sonia didn't want to disclose the fact that her late husband had named him as the trustee of his will.

"I see. He told me he wanted to see his friend's widow; but he was suddenly called away by a friend who lives in a small village about forty kilometres outside Delhi, as his wife had a heart attack. May be he'll come to see you tomorrow."

When Sonia returned from bhajan, she felt very peaceful. Her mother and Neena were sitting in the living room. She sat beside Neena who said,"Mom after you left, a driver brought a couple of bags belonging to Dad with a note from Dr. Khanna."

Sonia took the note from Neena and  read it.  "You know, Dr. Khanna is Radha's son."

"Radha is a nice person, I didn't know her son was back. I must congratulate her." Said Tara.

After the evening dinner, Sonia went to her bedroom. It was very hot. She opened her window. Later she took a cool shower and slipped into a comfortable kaftan. This casual wear softly moulded her figure. She looked very attractive.

A young widow in her late thirties, Sonia lived with her two children, Neena and Niel, in New Delhi, in Greater Kailash, in a house which was elegant and hinted of luxury.

Her son Niel had gone to Simla, like children of other rich families, to study in a resident school.

Sonia had not heard from Niel since he left a week ago. She was a bit worried about him.. Impulsively she picked up her children's album to look at his photos, when she heard a knock on her bedroom door. "Come in, the door is open."

Gopal, her servant, came in followed by a visitor. For a split second she failed to recognize him as he had grown a small beard. Then suddenly a prickle of awareness slithered down her spine when she saw him leaning against the wooden frame of the door, as years back she had seen him standing within the glass door of the dance hall, in London.

As she encountered a pair of tawny eyes levelled in her direction, she felt herself grow faintly pink beneath their gaze. The album dropped from her hand. He covered the short distance between them with a movement that was lithe and deliberately indolent; picked up the album and placed it on the table beside her.

Her mouth felt dry. For several seconds she didn't couldn't..say anything, remaining in her seat, staring at him through a mist of confusion.

It was K.K.she had no doubt about it, older of course. She could see lines etched upon his features which had not been there ten years back when she danced with him and spent quite a few hours with him at the party.

She was confused as to what he was doing in India. She saw his eyes rove over her features with dismaying thoroughness before coming to rest on her mouth.

"Hello," she murmured, meeting his dark,probing gaze squarely.

"It took you a long time to recognize me. Have I changed that much in all these years?"
A brow lifted in mock enquiry. Then he smiled and added," I would have recognized you any where."

Without conscious thought her eyes slid down to his mouth and a tiny shiver shook her equilibrium as she imagined the way those  sensuously moulded lips had caressed her skin ten years earlier.  She couldn't guess what K.K.must be thinking about her behind the cool mask he was presenting. She took a deep breath before she rose from her seat and said," What can I do for you?"

 His golden brown eyes were watching her action curiously. This brought a twisting smile of cynicism  to  the ruthlessly hard mouth; but the look he  directed  at her  was  smoothly without emotions as he spoke.

"This evening, I sent your husband's bags.  In one of them, I had put a few bottles of injectons which I forgot to take out. I've  come  for  those  as  I  need  them  immediately  for  my friend's wife, who just had a severe heart attack."
 The palm of Sonia's hands were beginning to become damp, and a cold chill ran down her spine at his words.
Her nervousness increased. She chided herself to  relax,  but she couldn't as the events of  that day  in London,  ten years ago, vividly came back to her.

*   *   *

 While they were dancing, he smiled at her and commented, "No rings?"

Sonia laughed and nodded. He gave her a quick warm smile and said, "Are you seldom in London? I haven't seen you around."

Sonia again smiled. She felt his intent gaze very disturbing.

Before she left the dance floor, he asked, "What is your name?"

"Sonia." Then a little reluctantly, she asked, "and what's yours?"    "They call me K.K. here."

* * *

Since she had lied to him deliberately, she felt ashamed of her behaviour. Now that he was here as trustee of her husband's will she wanted to justify her behaviour; but before she could say something, he said, "I couldn't have dreamt of seeing you here as Dr.Rajinder's widow. He never mentioned your name to me. I'm quite sure you indicated that you were unattached."

Sonia didn't answer. She picked up her keys and beckoned him to follow her. She took him to the adjoining room where Neena had placed the bags and handed him the keys.

He opened one of the bags, took out a small card-board box and stood there for a while looking at her. He was amazed to see that in these ten years, there was hardly any change in her appearance. In fact, he was looking into a perfect oval face, with clear black eyes, shining like two stars. The same aristocratic nose, broad intelligent forehead, tender and sensual lips. He found her still slim; and a special glow set her apart from most other women. Something in his manner had prevented Sonia from walking past him. She felt shaken and apprehensive.

Kanwal became aware of her emotions; so his hand closed

on the  soft flesh of her upper arm.

"You are trembling. Have I frightened you so much?" He said with a soft chuckle.

Sonia brushed her hand in front of her eyes and tried to steady herself.

"I'm really sorry for keeping back my identity then, as I was scared." She tried to justify herself.

"Perhaps we  were young and played games. Ten years do make a lot of difference in one's outlook," Kanwal said to put her at ease. Then added, "Well, it's been very nice seeing you, my dear. My patient needs all the attention, right  now."

"Good night,"  she managed  evenly as she closed the door.

It was only as she crept between the bed sheets a short while later that she allowed to dwell on the evenings events. She felt she couldn't get rid of her past. Lately she had tried to put it behind her; it was still threatening her present and future. Something about Kanwal made her feel afraid.... ...... why! She couldn't fathom. Again and again the memory of that evening when she danced with K.K. in London, kept her awake for a long time, before drifting into sleep.

In the morning as usual, Tripta, Sonia's personal maid, brought her tea in bed. The aroma awoke her. She sat up and held the cup from her.

"Did you have a nice sleep? "Tripta asked, seeing black circles around her mistress' eyes.

"I didn't sleep well," she said. Her mind was still in a turmoil. The hot cup of tea soothed her nerves and gradually she calmed down. After a cool shower when she returned to her room, Gopal brought two letters. She looked at them and handed one to him saying, "This one is for mother. Take it to her."

"Breakfast has been laid, Madam", Gopal said.

"Tell Neena to escort her grand mother to the dining room. I'll be there in a minute,"

Sonia's letter was from her husband's solicitor in London. It contained few details of the property and stated that Dr.Khanna was keen to discuss everything personally with her when he reached India.

When Sonia, her mother, and Neena were eating their breakfast, Tara said, "I just received a letter from Prem."

"What does Prem aunty write?"

"She's suggested a match for Neena. Her friend's son has recently returned from London after a barrister's degree. The boy Narinder is the only son. The father is a business man. They are not very rich; but the family is good."

"Mother, let Neena finish her internship. Do you think there'll will be dearth of good matches for her?  After all, she's not only rich, she's also a doctor."

"In a few months her internship will be over. Do you want her to start working after it?"

"I don't see any reason why she shouldn't work?" Sonia answered.

Neena who was quietly listening, guessed it was time to intervene.

She said, "Grandma, I'm still doing my internship and I would certainly like to get a little more experience, working for a few more years before I even start thinking of getting married."

Tara looked at her grand-daughter in surprise. "There's  no reason why you shouldn't get married as soon as possible. You've read your father's will. Do you want to lose your inheritance?"

Neena didn't answer. Tara again said, "You have no choice.

You've got to marry before you complete your twenty fourth year."

"And if I didn't?"

"You know quite well, your share of the property will be kept in trust with Dr. Khanna, till your brother comes to age, to inherit."

"Mother, let me think about it. Since Dr. Khanna is in India, let me discuss it with him." said Sonia.

"If you want it that way, that's fine with me. I'll write to Prem to wait for our decision." Then looking at Neena, Tara said, "I know what you are thinking. I agree I am old fashioned. Still, I'll advise you to give it a second thought."

To put a stop to this sensitive issue, Sonia said, " Aren't you going to the hospital?"

Neena looked at her wrist watch.,I guess I'm already late." Before she left, she looked at her grandmother and    said, "Thanks, grandma, for your suggestion. I'll think about it."

Once in her bedroom, Sonia opened the window for a breath of fresh air. Suddenly a movement among the trees near the house caught her attention. She saw K.K's tall figure emerge into the open ground and his long strides carried him swiftly towards the house. He stopped and raised his head and focused his gaze on the window where Sonia stood. Startled, she started to step back, then realized he couldn't possibly see her at that angle. She saw his mouth quirk at the corner as he continued to stare at the window.

A blush of self anger at her own stupidity roughed her cheeks when she realised what he must imply. Hastily she released the curtain and saw the amused upward curl of his mouth deepen.

Irritated by her own action,  she pivoted  impatiently away from the window.

The very fact that he had come to see her made her feel nervous. An inner voice told her she was becoming much too conscious of him, and would be very foolish to let him disturb the even tenor of her life. She couldn't afford to let him have the slightest edge over her. She was quite sure he didn't believe a word of the explanation she had given him last evening as to her behaviour in London when she had lied to him of being single.

A few minutes later Gopal announced his arrival. "Take him to the drawing room, I'll be there in a minute."

She wondered why Rajinder had made him trustee of his will. She had to find courage, some how, to make him understand. She didn't want her life to be disrupted. She was afraid because she knew his magnetism was utterly disarming. There was a certain danger in continuing an association with a man of his calibre. He possessed undoubted charm, an undeniable animal magnetism which had unbalanced her in London and could be difficult to resist in her present vulnerable circumstances.

Though Sonia's complexion needed no make up, still she looked into the mirror. Finding her face pale due to nervousness, she applied a little moisturising cream for a subdued glow and also a little eye shadow to intensify the colour of her eyes.

When she entered the drawing room, her heart began to beat crratically. For a few seconds she couldn't speak. It was as if her tongue was struck to the roof of her mouth.

Hearing her enter, Kanwal turned around. She met his slightly mocking smile as his eyes gleamed with devilish laughter.

In fact, it was his probing, disturbing manner that was responsible for her present anguish. He bore an air of assured sophistication.   His light grey suit was impeccably tailored, and his shirt of cream silk and an elegantly knitted tie were a perfect complement.

Once again the sight of that sensuously moulded mouth brought a vivid reminder of his passionate kiss. The memory made her shiver. She saw him intently studying her.

"Namastay *Bhabhiji,"** Dr.Khanna said, folding his hands in the Indian tradition. He was not sure about her after last night, so he had promised to be formal and call her bhabi,* being his friend's wife.

By then Sonia had composed herself. She spoke softly, "Please take a seat. Can you not call me Sonia, as I am the younger."

I didn't want to offend your mother." He said tactfully.

"I know she wouldn't mind."

"You too must call me K.K.or Kanwal." He said with a broad smile.

"How is your patient?"   Sonia asked, to change the subject.

"The injections last night worked a miracle. She is now out of danger."

They were still talking when Gopal brought tea and a few home made cookies, dry fruit and nuts. Sonia poured tea and handed him a cup. She made one for herself and sat quietly sipping.

"What are you thinking?" he asked.

"I'm sorry for my behaviour last evening", Sonia said truthfully.

"There's no need for apology. I had been so distraught, I came directly to your room. But I'm thankful I could save a life. A little more delay could have been fatal."

His steadfast gaze made her nervous again,  so she looked

* Wishing                              ** Sister-in-law

away, hastily wracking her mind for something to say, but before she could do so, Kanwal said, "I hope I wasn't late. I'm sorry if I made you wait for me any extended length of time."

"I wasn't watching you at the window, if that's what you are implying." Declared Sonia a little haughtily, as she was upset for her own stupidity. Then giving herself a mental shake she said changing the subject, "When did you last see Rajinder?"

"On the eve of his departure to India. To tell you the truth I feel guilty for his death."

"Why do you say that?" He died in an air accident, "she elaborated."

"I know. It was on my persuasion that he left England to come and see you and find a solution, a compromise."

"I'm not sure, I understand you.,"Sonia said with eyes downcast.

Kanwal looked at her for a long time. He was debating within himself. Should he believe she  was as innocent as she appears?  She had lied to him in London when she said she was single. Suddenly another thought crossed his mind. It was so unlike him to fall in love at first sight at that dance. After that evening, he had been looking for her all over London for quite a few months before he gave up his search. Seeing a frown on his face, Sonia couldn't resist asking. "Is something wrong?"

Then with a calm and cool voice he said, "Let me put it this way. On the eve of Rajinder's departure to India, I was with him. He had invited me over to play chess. He was very unhappy. During the game he confessed his inability to concentrate due to over drinking."

"That doesn't answer my question," Sonia said with impatience.

Kanwal was hesitant. For a few seconds he looked into his tea cup collecting his thoughts before he spoke, "Would you mind if I asked you a personal question?"

"Try me."

"Why did you come back to India after Niel's birth? Did Rajinder do something you felt to be wrong, having you artificially in...semi........?"

Before he could complete his sentence, Sonia blurted out, "So you know I was artificially inseminated."

"Was that the reason you left England?"

"No, there were other reasons too. " She said automatically.

Kanwal who knew that Rajinder was impotent, had a curious feeling as to who was Neena's father. May be she had a lover in India and wanted to come to him. This brought a cynical smile as he looked at her. To his utter amazement he saw two tears glide down her cheeks.

He came to sit beside her and wiped them."I hope you trust me?. Would you like to unburden yourself?"

Sonia nodded. She took a deep breath to stabilize herself. How could she tell him she had been unhappy with her life and so had succumbed to his charms in just two meetings in London.

"The day I met you at the dance hall, I was upset.When I saw you I was anxious to get rid of the man who was coming on to me."

"Was it Varinder by any chance?" asked Kanwal.

"How do you know ?"

"I saw him standing close to you. Why was he pursuing you?"

"Earlier he had asked me to dance, but I found his behaviour undesirable. I told him to take me back to a table as I felt nauseated. Instead, he forcibly took me to the garden and shocked me when he said that he was the bio-logical father of my son Neil. He also made a pass at me. I evaded his clutches and ran inside.

He also threatened to take my son away from me if I didn't toe his line. This scared me, and I left England at the first opportunity."

"I'm not sure if Rajinder knew about this development."

* * *

Sonia remembered having confronted her husband the very next day, to explain why he got her artificially inseminated without her consent. On his admitting that he was impotent, she was alarmed. It was then that she realized Neena was the product of rape on her wedding night in the train.

* * *

The memory choked her voice but soon she collected herself and fixing her eyes on Kanwal she said, "I did tell Rajinder about it."

Sonia saw Kanwal's expression momentarily soften. "I'm sorry if I hurt your feelings," he said, putting his arms around her. Sonia wasn't prepared for the strange curling sensation that began in the pit of her stomach, when he put his arm around her. It slowly spread until her whole body felt tinglingly alive.

There was a sheer physical magnetism she had thought herself not capable of experiencing again after all these years. A shiver of apprehension slid down her spine as she endeavoured to move away from him.

Kanwal's lips twisted into a slight smile, then let his gaze rove over her attractively attired form. "I can't figure out why Rajinder made me trustee of his will. He never mentioned that to me."

"I guess he decided it suddenly, as he sent this information to his lawyer only from the airport."

"I'm here to find out what I'm supposed to do, to help you. Rajinder has left the entire responsibility of his family to me." Kanwal also showed Sonia the letter he had received through his lawyer.

Sonia sat quietly before she spoke, "since Neena is the one who is really effected, you'll have to talk to her." Then she added, "My aunt has suggested a good match for Neena but she doesn't like the idea of getting married so soon. I guess you'll have to make her understand its importance; to get the will executed."

"I've taken a lot of your time. I should be leaving. I'll phone Neena and come and see her sometime."

In the evening Neena came to her mother's room. She wanted to find out all about Dr.Khanna. "What did Dr.Khanna say?"

"He'll phone you sometime tomorrow and come and  see you to discuss any problem you have." Then added very softly, "Your grandma hasn't come out of her room the whole day. You hurt her feelings. Why don't you go and apologise?"

"I'm sorry if I hurt her feelings. But can't you see what I'm trying to say? please tell grandma to give me sometime to think it over; after all it's my life."

"I don't want  to rush you in it; but is there any harm in meeting the boy and his family? If you don't approve of them, we can always refuse their offer. I'm sure your grandma will be quite willing to go along with you."

"Mom, I don't want to get married so soon."

"If your father was alive we could have argued with him to get your way. I really can't figure out why he put such a clause in the will? Do you think your marriage would interfere with your work?"

"Who knows what kind of a partner I'll have?"

"We are running short of time; if there is some one else in your life, I can certainly look up the family."

Neena kept quiet. Suddenly she thought of Mohan, her class mate. She always enjoyed his company. Yet she was not sure about her feelings for him.

"Mom, I'm really greatful for your consideration. I don't think I'm interested in any one."

They were still talking when the telephone started ringing. Neena picked up the receiver. "Yes, mom is here. Would you like to talk to her?"

Sonia got the receiver and talked to Radha. After exchanging pleasantries, Sonia said, "mother has other engagements and I'm not sure about Neena. I'll let you know later, but thanks for inviting."

Sonia put down the receiver and said, "Mrs. Khanna has invited us to a party she's giving at her place tomorrow evening. Do you want to go?"

Since her husband's death, Sonia had stopped attending any parties. Neena had been trying to persuade her but to no avail. Knowing about the invitation, Neena said, "Mom, you've been out of circulation since dad died. Why don't you attend this one. This will also give me a chance to know Dr.Khanna and talk to him."

Neena looked very anxious, so Sonia reluctantly had to agree.

At night in bed Sonia felt too scared to face Kanwal, because his mere nearness set her heart racing, and affected her. One part of her wanted nothing to do with this inimically compelling man, and yet she longed for the joy of love......the strength of emotions that bound a man and a woman together for a life time.

She wanted it more than anything; being deprived of that joy in her early life.


## CHAPTER II


Neena was dressed for the party. She looked very attractive in a pink chiffon saree with a sleeveless matching blouse. A small golden chain with a solitaire diamond adorned her neck. She looked as tall as her mother.

Knawal rang the bell."come in, Dr.Khanna," Neena said, as she answered the door. He shook hands with her,"Glad to meet you Neena," "Thank you."

In the drawing room Neena asked him to take a seat."Mom is getting dressed. She'll take a few more minutes. Could we talk till then?"

"Of course."

"According to my father's will, I should get married before I complete my twenty fourth birthday. Could that clause be over looked?"

"No, you can't. I talked to your attorney in London. He insisted that clause in the will was quite clear. You have to get married accordingly."

Then added,"I don't see any reason why you shouldn't marry, now that you've completed your education. Sonia tells me that her aunt has suggested a good match."

"I don't want to get married so soon. I want to work."

"You can certainly work after you're married."

"Suppose my husband doesn't want me to work?"

"That's past history. I assure you, no man would be  stupid

enough not to let a doctor work, unless there is a problem."

"But I'm against arranged marriages."

"That's understandable. What about our culture? You know even love marriages don't work all the time. Think in terms of your inheritance, and only then decide."

They were still talking when Sonia came to the door. Seeing her enter, Kanwal stood up. Sonia saw his tall frame outlined with startling clarity against the light and her heart missed a beat.

Kanwal looked at her. She was wearing a silk saree in soft tones of beige, cream and brown that fell in graceful folds from a gathered waistline, a sleeveless cream silk blouse and elegant sandals in matching beige, that made her look very attractive. He came close to her and folding his hands said, "Namastay Sonia. If you're ready, let's go."

Sonia was nervous. Her stomach had started behaving in a nervous fashion. She wanted to plead headache and decline to go, Kanwal sensed it; for he calmly reached out and caught hold of her arm. She couldn't do anything else. She started walking quietly by his side to the car. In the car she sat in silence, aware of the broad tanned hand on the gear shift, the quiet strength of the man at her side. Sonia wanted to just close her eyes and lean back...pretend the past didn't exist. She would then like to meet his eyes and smile, to respond freely without fear or inhibition. Suddenly another thought overpowered: what would it take to ruffle that seemingly inflexible composure? She'd seen anger flare briefly in those tawny gold eyes when he first came to her room. Instincts warned her that when aroused it would be swift and deadly.

Kanwal drew up in front of the porch of a two storey bungalow with wide lawns full of flowers. He stepped out and went round to open Sonia's and Neena's doors. Sonia couldn't help thinking Kanwal looked magnificent, wearing dark trousers and a polo necked black body shirt that showed his muscles.

Kanwal led them to a big drawing room with a deep red carpet, specially designed in Iran.

Sonia's eyes sparkled with appreciation and admiration. Every piece of furniture was elegant.

Radha welcomed them. Sonia sat down on the couch. Kanwal too sat down close to her. She found his proximity was making her nervous; he had only to move fractionally towards her and they would touch. She came out of her reverie when she heard Kanwal say, "Would you prefer tea or a cold drink.?"

"Tea would do," she said nervously.

Ranjit, the man servant, came in with a tray of tea and some hot pakoras. Kanwal took the tray and put it on a side table.

Neena came forward to pour tea. She filled the cups and handed one to each of them, then filled one for herself.

As soon as Kanwal put down his own cup her mother said, "Why don't you go and change for the party? Its time for other guests to arrive."

"It's very hot today; so we have a swimming program before the party starts. The pool is not very far from the house; You do swim, don't you?" asked Radha.

Actually, I don't know much." Sonia replied self-consciously. By then the suffocating tension that had enveloped Sonia, seemed to leave the room, with Kanwal. She hadn't realized how stiffly she had been holding herself until she drew a free breath on his departure.

Sonia and Neena followed Radha. She led them through the

garden behind the bungalow to the pool, where there were gaily coloured beach umbrellas, several brightly coloured chaise lounges, and numerous tables and chairs. Shrubs in painted wooden tubs were spaced to provide contrasting colour, and there were bananas, palms and decorative pebbles gardens flanked by a take away bar and restaurant. The effect was distinctly tropical and designed to encourage guests to enjoy the party.

The guests had started to arrive. Sonia saw Kanwal, in a grey suit and a white shirt with a black bow tie, welcoming them. The suit fitted his muscular leanness perfectly. The very thought brought colour to her cheeks so she made a pretence of straightening the lapel of her saree.

Neena saw two of her friends arrive; so she left Sonia with Radha to join them.

It was a hot summer day. Kanwal requested all his guests to join in a game of water-polo in the swimming pool. They were told to find bathing suits or trunks in the closets of their respective changing rooms. Those guests who were reluctant to swim, sat drinking and relaxing.

Radha led Sonia to a table; but before they sat down Kanwal, accompanied by his friend Dr. Sohan Singh and his french wife Loren came there. He introduced them to Sonia. Sonia who could speak french fluently, started talking to Loren. They were still talking when Kanwal and Dr.Sohan Singh, now in their swimming trunks, joined them.

"Loren, aren't you going to have a swim?" asked her husband. "Yes, we'll follow you."

As soon as Dr.Singh jumped into the pool, Loren said," Shall we go and change?"

A few minutes later, appropriately clad, Sonia and Loren went to the edge of the pool where Kanwal and  Sohan Singh were swimming. Sonia saw Kanwal's lean body cutting the water in a fast crawl down the length of the pool. Soon he and Dr. Singh reached the spot where Loren and Sonia were standing, ready to jump.

Kanwal's gaze strayed towards Sonia. He couldn't help feeling that she was a beautiful woman, looking hardly old enough to have two grown up children. Her legs were still shapely, her slim round hips curved into a slender waist.

Loren jumped in and started swimming beside her husband. Sonia followed her. After a few strokes, she slowed down and turned back. Seeing this, Kanwal was beside her.

Sonia became too conscious of him attired in hip hugging briefs that exposed his long muscular thighs, a broad chest covered with dark hair, and well muscled shoulders. He exuded virile masculanity.

"How about my helping you to swim in the deep?"

"Thank you, I'll stay where I am. Please don't bother." She said, aware that his voice had the power to turn her into a spineless wreck, and to trust him to be close to her, spelled sure disaster, and which her emotions couldn't hope to cope with.

"You have nothing to fear so long as I am by your side. I'm sure you'll overcome your fear, once you start swimming in the deep water." He said as he came close to her, trying to be a perfect host.   Sonia's senses were already clamouring too loudly and his touch set her heart racing. She saw the tanned breadth of his uncovered shoulders, his chest bare except for the mat of hair that marched down to the naval.

Kanwal was aware of Sonia's eye on him. He had deliberately put his hands on her shoulders and swept her with him towards the deep end.

In her fright, Sonia had pressed so close to him,    that her breasts were soft cushions against his chest and her thighs touched his as she entwined her legs around him.

Sonia blushed crimson as her eyes flicked up to his, then, collecting courage, she started swimming again.

She had gone a little distance when she saw Kanwal had fallen behind. In panic, she plunged towards him and flung her arms around his neck. Kanwal threw back his head and burst out laughing. The deep heavy sound was so contagious that mirth played with the corners of Sonia's mouth until she too began to laugh, still holding on to him. Suddenly Kanwal took hold of her chin and then his mouth was closing over hers. That seductive fire consumed her once again. She wanted to go on drowning in the sensual oblivion of his caress. From the admission, came the strength to resist. With a tremulous gasp, she twisted away from his mouth using her hands to wedge a space between them. Her skin felt hot to touch, the raging fire within refusing to slow down. Then with a single fluid movement she was out of his hold, trying to swim away.

Kanwal made no move to follow her. As soon as she reached the shallow end, he resumed swimming; seemingly relaxed and undisturbed. Sonia was out of the pool. The initial shock of the physical contact, she just had with his muscled chest made her mind spin. Her chest constricted sharply; her bright eyes darkening to mirror the unendurable pain she felt. Her voice was choked by the knot in her throat. Without answering Loraine as to why she was out so soon, she hurried to the changing room. She wished she had never met him or been momentarily entranced by his handsome looks, in London. She was convinced he was a passionate man For all his impassive exterior, a man of the elements...primitive, ruthless and strong.

Sonia was determined not to give him a single indication that she was interested in him as anything more than her late husband's friend. She decided to look at him squarely and not flinch under his gaze. With this determination she got dressed and walked towards the second lounge where Radha was sitting.

The sun was dipping into the western horizon and looked like a big crimson fire ball. Most of the guests had left the pool and were dressing for the party.

Kanwal changed into a long sleeved silk shirt, predominantly white with a design in beige and cream. The top buttons were undone, revealing dark, curling hair glistening from swimming. He came and stood close to his mother and looking at Sonia asked, "Can I get you a drink?"

"No," she snapped.

As Radha looked curiously in her direction, she hesitantly and softly added. "Thank you, any way."

"How about going to the inner lounge? Its rather warm here. I'll be with you in a minute." said Radha, then added,"Please, do have something cold to drink."

"Please, come through to the lounge," Kanwal bade amiably, the attentive host, and Sonia reluctantly allowed herself to be led across the wide hall.

Sonia watched as Kanwal crossed to the drink cabinet, and her eyes followed the smooth actions, his hands effected. She sat sipping her drink close to him, but as more guests came in, she lost sight of him. When she eventually rediscovered him, he was standing talking and serving champagne to his friend's wife in the centre of the lounge. Music was played and guests had started dancing.

* * *

Sonia was deep in thoughts of a similar party, where she

had danced with Kanwal. Of course she was then young. Her husband had left her there while he went with his associate, Dr.Astra, to the laboratory. Sonia was angry at his behaviour; so she freely dnced with all the young doctors without being properly introduced.

* * *

Her trance was broken when a hand lightly touched her arm. She looked up and saw Kanwal. The grooves around his eyes and mouth deepened when he said, "How about a dance?"

Sonia caught her breath, hesitating and yet quite aware of the compelling mastery of the man as he stood close to her, his face smiling and his profile obdurate.

"Why don't you dance  with some one else. I'm too rusty now."

"I don't think so," he said quietly. He curved his arm about her waist and took her hand. Kanwal led her into the first step; but he could feel her nervous tension. As the dance progressed, he felt her muscles relax and then the old rhythm came back, and they glided around the floor with grace.

Kanwal's lips curved slowly into a warm smile and assumed a gentleness when he said, "do you remember how we enjoyed dancing in London that night?"

"Yes, she murmured shyly."

Sonia and Kanwal looked like a well matched couple. Her five feet seven, fitted nearly against him. While dancing his gaze swept appraisingly over her. He couldn't help saying, "you are beautiful. I still find no change in you."

Sonia's heart beat quickened at his compliment. She was caught unaware as she looked up at him. His eyes seemed to bore into her soul. She tried to  draw  her own away  but they were held as if by magic spell. An electric current seared through her body.

The firm pressure of Kanwal's hands at her back made it easy for her to follow his lead. With each step she became more fluid, her rigidity yielding to the challenge of his natural grace. Sonia tried hard to strain slightly against his arm so she wouldn't be pressed too closely against his hips.

When Sonia looked up, she was caught once more by the golden brown eyes so like those of both her children, in which she always felt she saw a lazy, feline arrogance.

There was a strange, haunted quality that had suddenly deepened her eyes and lent a pensive air to her expressive features. Kanwal saw it. "Is something wrong?" he asked deliberately.

Sonia didn't answer. It pained her that she had no idea who fathered both her children. She just looked up and smiled as she dared not give out her secret. They were still dancing when the lights dimmed, announcing the entertainment. People scrambled to their chairs as a slow roll began on the drums.

Kanwal still had his arms around her as they too sat down and watched the spotlight circle the room. Sonia was crushed so close to him at their crowded table that she could feel his every movement against her own body. A thundering discovery vibrated over her with the sudden awareness of a summer storm. It was something with similar movements of the unknown person in her past. This shocked her, and then she put those thoughts away from her as absurd and a figment of her imagination. It was true that something had been troubling Sonia ever since the first time she had seen him at the library in London. Some little something that set him apart from any man she had ever known.

After the entertainment of the folk dancers, people drifted towards the supper tables. Kanwal proved a generous and a considerate host, helping the guests enjoy their meal.

Sonia sat beside Radha, trying to make small talk.

She was actually interested to know about Kanwal's earlier years, and what he was like a boy; because whenever he was close to her, she had a curious feeling she had met him somewhere. She decided to find out as much as she could about him from his mother. However she suggested to herself that there was no reason to suppose he looked upon her as anything other than his friend's wife, and she wanted to keep it that way. as she still bore the scars from one encounter so why invite another headache? In spite of all her reasoning, while sitting and talking to Radha, Sonia's sensitive radar never lost track of where Kanwal was in the big hall. Invariably her gaze would follow him.

A few minutes later Sonia saw Kanwal entertaining a beautiful lady. She couldn't resist studying the exquisitely feminine features of his friend... features that could change from sensually alluring to... suddenly there was a dismaying flutter in her breast as she saw him being warmly kissed. She tried not to watch as misery tightened her throat. She wished fiercely for the lady to leave.

Sonia didn't know why she was feeling jealous. She suggested to herself that Kanwal was a man of the world. He had lived, all his life, in a country where kissing was a normal feature of greeting. Moreover at his age he wouldn't have been normal if he hadn't sought feminine companionship. But the lady in question seemed to be making it fairly obvious that, at some time or other, they had shared an intimate relationship. Soon she saw her leaving. Her cheery departing wave was returned by a look that was broodingly thoughtful. This puzzled Sonia. Absently her hand reached up, separating a strand of dark hair from the others to twist it around her finger.

Kanwal noticed her sitting by herself, and as a perfect host, he was by her side. "I guess my mother has left you on your own. You look as if you haven't eaten anything. I'll get you some food."

He took Sonia's hand and led her to the supper table. While she was filling her plate, his eyes examined her with disconcerting thoroughness. Sonia noticed it and felt sure her inner agitation must be quite apparent to him. She was helpless, for in spite of the table separating them, she felt the force of his masculinity.

Later in the evening, when Kanwal was escorting them home, his gaze was constantly falling on her. As they stepped out of the car, Kanwal said, "Namastay Sonia. Thank you for joining the party. Hope you enjoyed it?" He kissed Neena on the forehead and waited for them to go in door.

Sonia felt his eyes following their path to the door, before he got behind the wheel. His gaze flickered to her briefly before he reversed out of the drive way.

Sonia stood there for a while indecisively. It was quite obvious that he had given her a lot of attention. At the memory of that fleeting kiss in the swimming pool; a swift flood of colour tinged her cheeks, as she felt blood rushing. It was really mortifying as she couldn't prevent the slight trembling of her lips. She was certain about the undeniable physical attraction, was daily in-creasing; at the same time, she was not at all certain about him. To her, he was an enigma, so she decided to hide her feelings to herself.

Once in bed, sleep alluded her. She went over his suggestive remarks while dancing with her. The more she thought about them, the more she realized it had been an attempt to flirt with her. On a second thought she felt guilty of accusing him for his casual reference to her beauty; when she remembered those doctors in London, who complemented her, but she took their remarks very lightly as it didn't disturb her then.

Amid this turmoil of emotions, Sonia closed her eyes. When sleep came at last, she started dreaming. She was attending a party. She saw a tall man wearing a mask come to her side, asking her to dance. She didn't know who he was. She admired his dancing. Gradually he threaded his way towards the garden and forcibly put his mouth to hers. Sonia tried to get away from him, but he was holding her in his iron grip, as he snapped with cold and frightening eyes, "There's no one to protect you now."

Sonia was paralysed with fear. She tried to grip the table beside her. Soon she saw him removing his mask; but she couldn't see his face as he was in shade. She cried out for help, but no sound came out of her throat. She felt her heart was about to break, but she was beyond tears. When he tried to rape her, his very action made her scream. Suddenly she saw Kanwal. He moved swiftly, dragged the man to the other side of the garden and threw him down. For a full second, Sonia was only aware of his disturbing presence. He then held her softly in his arms, leaned forward and kissed her on the lips.

"Don't you think," holding her at a distance, he said mockingly, "you need a man's affection for the rest of your life. Do you want to remain a rich attractive widow, challenging men who want to win your favour? You are indeed very bewitching and desirable. I can't stop myself from kissing you."

Trapped in his steel like embrace, she felt his kiss vibrate through her whole body. Totally unable to resist, she clung to him and her hands were around his neck, fingers winding into the thickness of his hair as she fixed her eyes on his mouth feeling her heart beat quicken.

"Am I supposed to feel honoured now that you want me to make love to you? "He said in a soft, taunting voice.

At this Sonia's anger flared. Breathing heavily, she tried to run away from him to the terrace door. She suddenly opened her eyes, when Tripta, her maid servant gripped her arm firmly and started shaking her.

"I'm sorry for waking you up. I couldn't help, seeing you breathing so heavily as if you were running." Tripta said.

Sonia looked around bewildered, and sat up. Holding the cup of tea from Tripta she said, " Yes, I was trying to run in my dream; but my legs wouldn't move."

While sipping tea, Sonia tried to analyze her dream. She couldn't forget Kanwal's words: "Do you want to...remain a rich widow, challenging men, who want to....win your favour?"

She was out of her reverie when she heard her mother say, "Aren't you late for your meeting?"

Sonia looked at her watch. "Yes, I am. Those ladies must be cursing me. We have to go out distributing clothes to the poor."

At noon, when she returned home, Gopal gave her the message that Dr. Khanna had phoned.

"What did he say?"

"He didn't leave any message. He'll phone you back."

Sonia was about to leave the dining room after lunch when the telephone rang. She guessed it was Kanwal's, so she nervously picked up the receiver. Kanwal was on the line. He said, "You wanted me to go and meet the boy Narinder at

Kanpore. Well, I'm taking mother to visit Lord Krishna's shrines at Mathura." then a little hesitantly he said, "How about joining us on the trip? After Mathura, we'll visit Agra, and Simla; and on our way back we can halt at Kanpore."

Sonia didn't answer. She was puzzled. She didn't know what to say.

"Are you there, Sonia?" asked Kanwal.

"Thanks for your offer; but I'm not sure if I can come."

"The point is, I won't be available after that as I'll be leaving for Bombay soon after I come back."

"Can you hold for a moment? I'll go and talk to mother." Sonia put down her receiver and went to her mother's room.

"You don't have to worry about me or Neena," Tara said. "We can both look after ourselves. You must go. Radha is a shrewd person. She can judge better than you. Of course Kanwal can talk to the boy and his father. If he thinks the match is good for Neena, we can announce the engagement."

"I don't want to do anything without Neena's consent."

"You can invite the family to Delhi and let Neena meet the boy and his parents."

Reluctantly, Sonia agreed to join them on their sight seeing trip.

At five in the evening the limousine drew to a whispered halt in the drive way. Kanwal stepped out and rang the door bell.

Tripta answered the door. Sonia glanced over her shoulder and saw him come into the drawing room. As usual, she felt nervous. The palms of her hands were wet. How strange, she thought, wiping the perspiration on the hips of her dress. She was angry that this arrogant man had tricked her into taking the trip with him. She guessed he effected her more than she had realized.

## CHAPTER III

Sonia stepped into the car and sat down beside Radha, and greeted her, "Namastay, Mrs. Khanna. How do you do?"

"I'm fine, thankyou. Glad to see you Sonia. Please call me Radha," she said with a warm smile.

Kanwal followed Sonia at the back. His gaze swept appraisingly over her as the simple design of her saree gave her an air of innocent sophistication.

Meanwhile, Amrit Lal stowed her luggage into the trunk; then slipped behind the wheel as soon as Kanwal's valet, Ram Singh, and Radha's personal maid, Maya, took their seats.

Kanwal's closeness, his thighs touching hers, affected Sonia while on their way to Mathura; although Kanwal appeared very relaxed. He sat with his arms stretched negligently on the back of the seat, his hand only spare inches from her head. This tensed her further. For sometime, Sonia pretended an interest in the passing scenery.

"I see you are far away in thoughts?" Kanwal commented while stretching his legs to be more comfortable.

Sonia felt the touch of his eyes, but she kept her gaze centered on the scenery outside, when she replied, "Nothing. I was just enjoying the  scenery." then she too leaned back. Gradually she over came her nervousness by consoling herself that perhaps there was nothing behind Kanwal's invitation, so she decided to enjoy the trip.

Kanwal asked the driver to stop the car at Meerut and take them to a nice restaurant for supper since it would be late when they would reach Mathura.

The restaurant was neat and clean and well patronised.

The dinner was quite a liesurely event during which Kanwal maintained a companionable flow of conversation, and after a few  relaxing minutes, they once again resumed their journey.

Though Sonia set herself the task of being an amusing and talkative guest, some how she felt that Kanwal's mother seemed to notice every little gesture, every smile. By then she must have had the impression that their relationship was other than what it looked like; not because of what Kanwal did or said, but because of her own nervousness and lack of confidence to look straight at him. When ever she tried, her gaze would skitter away from the gleam of mockery in his eyes.

The light was beginning to fade as they reached Mathura. They drove up to the hotel in front of the manicured lawns surrounding the main building.

At the hotel, indicating the chairs in the lobby .he declared, "Perhaps you'll both like to sit down while I go and register. I'll join you in a few minutes."

As they emerged into the courtyard, they could see a large tiled pool at a distance, with tourist enjoying its coolness. "I'm feeling too hot, and the pool is quite tempting. Can we all go for a swim, right away?" Kanwal asked with his golden tawny eyes looking straight at Sonia.

"Only if Sonia agrees," Radha said quietly.

Sonia almost suspected a conspiracy between Kanwal and his mother; so she was up against their determination, which combined, was fast proving to be formidable.

"Why don't you, both go and swim," Sonia replied smoothly; "I just want to relax under the shower."

"Never mind I can always come back and swim.

We've got the rooms on the northern side," Kanwal  said. "I'll lead the way."

Early next morning, Sonia dressed herself in a fine muslin saree with a matching cotton blouse to keep herself cool. The morning breeze tempted her to walk in the garden beside the pool. She paused at the first step, her hand resting on the polished banister when she heard footsteps behind her.

"Out for a walk?" asked Kanwal, coming close to her.

"Yes, I was ready a bit early and thought of taking a walk in the garden," Sonia tried to speak casually.

"Mind if I join you?" He asked politely.

Sonia sensed amusement dominating his voice. She shrugged, and with an air of careless indifference said, "You are welcome."  She looked at him to find the hard mouth curve into a cynical smile.

Suddenly Sonia got the impression that he didn't like her; not because she was'nt as beautiful as the woman he must be used to, but because she had lied to him. It was because she was a woman, she held herself motionless. May be he was a woman hater; otherwise, how could he be a bachelor at his age. May be he vied them with contempt, using them to satisfy physical needs. But why?  Had he fallen in love with a woman in the past and had been rejected?

"Is something wrong, Sonia?" Again ridiculing amusement dominated his voice. "You are very quiet."

She didn't answer his question, instead asked, "what are we doing today?"

"I came to tell you to have an early breakfast as mother wants to visit Gokul where Lord Krishna spent His early childhood. and from there only  we'll leave for Agra, in the evening, to see the Taj *in full moon."

. * Taj Mahal

The drive to Agra was avery smooth It took only a few hours. Sonia was thankful that apart from a few brief words she offered, in direct reply to Kanwal's queries, she was able to leave the bulk of the conversation to Radha.

The car slowed to pull into the curb in front of the Sheraton Hotel. After giving his hand to his mother, Kanwal turned to face Sonia. The metallic glitter of his gaze shimmered over his face as the outside street light fell on him. Sonia darted a quick glance at him, and felt she couldn't take it any more without betraying her feelings. She wished with all her heart that the trip would be over very soon.

Kanwal went to register, while they waited for him in the lobby. Sonia couldn't resist watching his broad, well muscled frame exuding a forceful vitality.

The three rooms were adjacent to one another. After leaving his mother in her room, he led Sonia to hers. He opened the door, then stood aside for Sonia to enter. She met his smile as she passed him.

Before he went to his room, that was adjoining Sonia's, Kanwal said, "Our table is reserved for eight-thirty. there's no need to get changed, unless you particulary want to. I'll collect both of you at eight and have a drink in the lounge before dinner."

"Thank you, Kanwal" Sonia inclined warmly. As Kanwal disappeared into the adjoining room, she crossed towards her bedroom.

Sonia took a cool shower and then wore a light blue chiffon saree with a matching sleeveless blouse.

Though the dress was casual, it afforded a sophistication she felt needed when in Kanwal's presence.

When he knocked at her door, she was ready. He viewed her appearance with a warm smile. He too had changed his shirt and added a jacket: The total effect was one of disturbing masculinity.

The dining hall was circular, and the floor was paved in black and white marble squares. Black and white marble panelling covered the walls, while the shadowy ceiling had been decorated with a muted garden scene mural. The cluster of bulbs sparkling in dim golden globes didn't give out enough illumination for Sonia to see the details of the paintings hung on the walls. The snow white table covers, with sparkling china and cutlery enhanced its decor. The total effect was one of tasteful elegance.

The sight of the Taj Mahal was breath taking. It shimmered majestically, with the pure white marble exterior bathed in brilliant moonlight. It was awe-inspiring and all of them looked at it wide eyed, realizing it was an edifice of love and, as described by a historian, "A tear drop on the cheek of time."

Sonia, Kanwal and Radha felt at peace. The interior of the Taj Mahal was as beautiful as its exterior. The workmanship was superb. They also went around the tomb of Shah Jehan, the Mughal Emperor, who had this memorial built for his beloved queen Mumtaj Mahal, who lay buried at his side.

Radha felt tired. She sat down on the marble bench in front of the Taj along with Maya. "Don't you want to see the rest of it?" Kanwal asked his mother. "I have been here several times. I'll rest here, but why don't you both go around?"

Sonia followed Kanwal around the lush green gardens, and passed rows of cypress trees bordering the fountains spraying and sparkling among the multicolored bulbs encircling every spout. Sonia felt at peace and responded to the restful atmosphere. The natural beauty of the place overcame her senses, and she couldn't help exclaiming!

"what a lovely sight! No matter how many times you come here, it's always soothing."

"It must be the music of the water and the purity of the marble edifice that soothes," Kanwal said leaning back against the tree, on the green grass near the fountains. His striking powerful features were fully illuminated by the moonlight. The unwavering study of his golden brown eyes made Sonia vividly aware of the primitive charm he possessed.

"It is really peaceful here, she said once again. "Perhaps Shah Jehan's love  for Mumtaj Mahal surrounds us and brings peace," said Kanwal and soon he crept closer to her.

Sonia's emotions were constantly at war where he was concerned. Out of desperation, she ventured, with face flushed and eyes over bright, "Let's get back.. it's getting late. Your mother....must be feeling... bored sitting...there for..s..s..s...so long." She stumbled over the words in her agitation, seeing the look in Kanwal's eyes. Suddenly Sonia gave a strangled gasp as Kanwal caught hold of her hand and spread her fingers between his own. Sonia disentangled her hand and tried to put as much space as quickly as possible, but his hands once again held hers.

The atmosphere became still between them, smiles leaving Sonia's face as his eyes held her captive. Her breath caught in her throat as she tried to break away from the intensity of that gaze. Lean hand moved out and slowly pulled her up and into a firmly muscled chest. He turned her around to face him, and then his mouth was on hers, warm and gently probing, parting her lips. His touch was disruptively sensual as he deepened the embrace, taking full advantage of her vulnerability trapped as she was in his arms.

Sonia felt her body melt at the intimacy of his touch, feeling his warmth through the thinness of her cotton blouse. The kiss set her on fire and turned her limbs into a shaky jelly-like substance incapable of holding her upright. An electric current shivered through her as she gave convulsive movement that served to excite him more. She groaned into his mouth as her nipple tautened against his palm.

Suddenly reaction set in, and she lashed out with her fists, her feet, but all to no avail. Kanwal simply drew her close against his hard frame, sliding one hand behind her head to hold it firm, while the other arm carved down her back.

"Oh, no," she protested, as she struggled desperately and pulled away from him.

Kanwal held her arm and looked down at her in the dim light of a near by lamp. "Hey," he chided softly. "Nothing happened." He reassured her.

She remained pale as he let go of her arm.     Her hand rubbed the chilling goose flesh on her upper arm. "No...yes...I suppose so," she sighed and heaved heavily against the tree. She pressed two fingers against her forehead, trying to rub away the throbbing ache that had started between her eyes.

She knew nothing had happened, except in her mind. God, how she had wanted, had never known such an instantaneous desire, her body still trembling with it.  "For God's sake," he snapped, I just kissed you, as I did in London. Then you didn't object. I didn't rape you." he said angrily.

Her gaze slid to him, still visibly trembling from the encounter. By then Sonia had calmed down a little. She guessed that Kanwal had stayed in the west so long that he couldn't have realized what he was doing. But in frustration she said, "I've been without male company for the last ten years. And you know how a woman alone is apt to see  more into these things than she should."

"I don't believe that any more than you do," he sighed, "although I'm sorry that such a fleeting kiss has caused such a hassle."

Once at the hotel, Kanwal left her at her door saying, "We leave for Simla at eight in the morning."

At night, Sonia found it difficult to sleep. She didn't know quite what he wanted from her; certainly a physical relationship, perhaps he also seemed to demand more than that. wanted her emotions to be involved as well as her body. After years of suppressing both, she couldn't give him either because she didn't want to get hurt again. She cursed herself for her own behaviour,  while in his arms. She felt helpless. Most disturbing of all was her reaction to the pressure of warm lips moving erotically against her own, her senses quickening, the arms that had gone up about his neck; and the fingers in the thickness of his hair. She was actually enjoying the physical contact with this wildly attractive man, in spite of her protest.

Suddenly she felt tired of all this soul searching. She guessed she had nothing to reproach herself about, no reason to feel guilty just because she was attracted to him. At the same time, another thought, that she had firmly put Kanwal in his place made her feel better. She once again justified herself by saying, "He has no right to come along and turn my life upside down this way."

That night Sonia awoke in the early morning hours when a vivid reminder of the rape returned in nightmare form to taunt her. She couldn't sleep after that, and took a cool shower and got dressed for the journey to Simla.

It was still early when she heard a knock on her door. As she opened the door she  saw Kanwal. "May I come in? he asked with a soft smile. Seeing Kanwal at the door, tinted Sonia's skin, but she managed to regard him steadily. For a moment she hesitated, then she stepped aside to let him enter. Kanwal's tawny eyes watched her with patient humour before he stepped in. Sonia closed the door behind her and stood a little shaken near her bed.

"I'm sorry about last night. Perhaps it was the surroundings that were responsible for my behaviour."

Sonia had a good upbringing. She didn't want to throw that away on him to whom she was no more than just a conquest. She wanted to end it all. He had succeeded in humiliating her last night, but she was going to act as if nothing had happened between them, mainly not for her own satisfaction; but also because Radha was an astute lady and wouldn't fail to notice any strain between K.K. and herself.

"Sonia," Kanwal prompted impatiently at her preoccupation. She forced herself to look at him, fighting the ridiculous colour that warmed her cheeks. Before she could say something, she felt Kanwal's finger tips gently on her lips as he silenced her. "You don't have anything to fear from me, Sonia. I am your late husband's friend, and have promised to look after you and your family."

Sonia couldn't answer him. She met Kanwal's eyes for a moment, then moved abruptly and walked off.

By noon they had reached Ambala. Kanwal seemed very relaxed, yet there emanated from him an aura of sensuousness and virility so strong as to be overpow-ering. Sonia couldn't resist stealing sideways looks at him through her long lashes. She guessed this man possessed power, intelligence, experience and confi-dence. It marked him as a man to be viewed with respect, but in her hearts of heart, she knew she could rely on his sincerity. These thoughts made her feel better.

At a convenient restaurant when they stopped for lunch, Sonia caught glimpses of their table in a long wall mirror. She was taken aback at an unexpected softness in her own face, her dark eyes smiling at him as he talked, her small dark head tilted in amusement. After lunch they drove on in complete silence. Sonia remained cool, determined not to succumb to the charm of his smile.

At night, they stayed at a hotel in Chandigarh, before proceeding to Simla.

The sun was not yet high in the sky when they started for Kalka. The country side had a look of dew filled freshness. On both sides of the road, fields stretched far and wide. Amid them one could see a few thatched huts, or a well worked by bullocks.

Gradually the scenery changed with citrus orchards lining on both sides. The hanging fruit seemed large and brightly yellow against the green trees. Far away one could look at the mountains on the horizon looming against the sky.

At Panjore gardens, they stopped for a while to flex their legs and get some lunch. Kanwal asked his valet to get some Channa *Bathura or Puri,* whatever was available. Mean while Kanwal asked his mother if she would like to go around the garden as it was a historical garden worth seeing, as it tells you lot about the Mughal Kings who were fond of gardens. Then holding his mother's arm he led her towards the garden while Sonia started to walk away through the trees for a breath of fresh air.

After a while Kanwal's mother sat under the shade of a tree. "I'll enjoy sitting here. You better go along with Sonia."

Kanwal soon caught up with her. When he held  Sonia's
    * Chick peas.     * kind of roti.

hand to help her over a puddle, she was furious at the reaction of her own body. Around the park the traffic swirled thickly, but beneath the trees the peace and brightness of the morning held promise of refreshment.

Kanwal had a lazy, casual way of doing everything, but Sonia sensed beneath that easy air an enormous dynamism, as if the silken cloak of his manner hid a terrible power.

A breath of summer wind blew through the trees sending a flickering diamond pattern over her face, and giving her hair a shifting brightness. They both strolled near the fountains with their curving jets, and across the long line of cypress trees that stood like sentinels guarding the beauty of the lush green gardens.

Within half an hour they were back where Radha sat on the bench. By then Ram Singh had brought the packed lunch from the restaurant.

they ate in comparative silence, the atmosphere peaceful between them. The accustomed tension of Kanwal's presence when he and Sonia were in the same room seemed to have seeped away after his assurance to her. Sonia felt at home, her mind and body relaxed.

At Kalka they halted just for a few minutes for a cup of tea, then they were again on their way to Simla. Beyond Kalka they entered hilly country, and Sonia's gaze, enthralled into patches of forests. The trees grew close there that one walking through them couldn't see the sky.

Away beyond these forests Sonia could see the fertile slopes on the hills. She remained glued to she window, watching the trail that led off through the forests. The road had begun to twist and turn as it rose and fell, and at each point the view was different. She saw grooves of trees looking out on small ribbons, like pools of glimmering water. There were also some well-kept gardens in front of the village houses, with begonias, chrysanthemums, dahlias, and roses in bloom.

A little further, in the ditches, she saw rosy hips dangling like polished gems on bare, black, arching branches. Sonia saw a range of hills towards which she thought they were going. As the mist began to disperse and float away like diaphanous chiffon scarves, the mountain side in all its glorious colours lay revealed.

She could see tall oaks, dark sage green hollies, and golden leaved birch growing in clusters a little away from the road side.

On the hills above, Sonia saw winding paths bordered by saffron tinted bracken that led downstairs to where a ribbon of a river cascaded from rocky ledges. A little distance from there, the car turned off the main road into a short, tree lined drive.

While Sonia was thus absorbed, Kanwal put his arm around her. She looked at him and her heart missed a beat. Then the car halted before an elegant bungalow.

Sonia waited for Kanwal to open the door. He held her arm to help her step out. Standing on the door step beside him, she looked up in admiration at the bright flower boxes which enlivened the window sills. the reds, yellows and purple of the petunias blazing against the white wood work of the tall windows. "it's lovely," Sonia said. "Thank you," said Kanwal, looking at her gently. Then he took his mother's arm. "You must be tired. You need to relax."

While Kanwal got his mother settled, Sonia wandered around the garden. Far above the garden Sonia saw the towering face of rock where the stream broke through and hurled itself down to the lake, sending a fine spray to cover her. The lake was just behind the bungalow. Her spell was broken to find Kanwal watching her with an amusing look.

"Would you like to go to your room to relax and change?" he asked politely. "You must be excited to go to meet Niel."

Sonia followed Kanwal, his stride long and powerful, muscles rippling beneath his shirt as he swung the double door open. Sonia knew he was a man who always had supreme self confidence.

The drawing room was very long, and had an air of comfortable elegance. One end was obviously the sitting area, which had an unobtrusive floral pattern, and the curtains at the long windows too were matching the pattern exactly. Under one of the windows was a rose wood desk fitted with books. At the other end of the room, there was a raised dias with a divan and two oblong round cushions with silken covers also matching the curtains. A few low chairs were grouped by the fire place and the wooden floor was covered with a priceless rug.

It was the painting of a pretty slender girl on the wall that held Sonia's attention. She looked very much like her Neena. "It's my grand-mother," Kanwal said.

The bedroom where Kanwal took her to, was also elegantly furnished as the rest of the house. The carpet was creamy and fluffy. The deep pink bedspread and velvet curtains at the windows matching perfectly, and the furniture a light pine.

Her suit case had already been placed on the ottoman at the bottom of the double bed. "The room is beautiful. Thank you, Kanwal."

"You are welcome, Sonia." saying this he came close and held her hand. The touch sent a wild flutter along her pulse. She looked up, off balance, and their eyes met. Kanwal made a sound under his breath and pulled her closer. Sonia was tempted to raise her mouth, but she quickly moved away. Kanwal's eyes showed pain for a brief moment. "I'm sorry," he said distantly. A strange expression flickered briefly across his face. I'll see you at tea time," and then he was gone.

Sonia watched him go in dismay. He had been attempting to be friendly, and she had perhaps bungled it. She knew he felt more for her than a fleeting attraction, and no matter how kind or good he was to her, she daren't assume anything.

Sonia remembered what Kanwal had said while dancing in London years back, and she had herself felt it at lunch on their way to Simla when she glimpsed the intimacy and communion of their bodies from a distance in the mirror, that confirmed the truth, they were creatures of the same world, their chemistry and natures oddly dovetailing.

By four o'clock Sonia was ready to go and meet Niel. There was a knock at her door. "Come in. The door is open." she said.

It was Kanwal, immaculately dressed. "Shall we go down to have our tea, before we leave?"

Kanwal held out his hand; but Sonia intentionally ignored it and turned too suddenly to descend the stairs. As her foot went down, she screamed as she toppled over. Kanwal some how managed to stop her before hitting the bottom of the stairs, pulling her hard against him. "Are you all right?" he murmured against her lips when he gave her a fleeting kiss.

"I'm all right now." she swallowed hard, pain in her dark eyes. She looked furious.

Kanwal's eyes widened at the injustice of her behaviour. Then he suddenly began to smile, the smile turning into a full throated laugh, with obvious enjoyment at her embarrassment.

Sonia was breathing hard, too furious to notice how handsome he looked. His genuine humour made him appear younger than his thirty seven years. With a cleft in one of his cheeks, he continued to smile, showing his very white teeth against his dark skin, and his eyes a tawny gold.

He sobered with an effort. "You look like a little girl when you are angry." Kanwal began to smile again.

This time Sonia did notice how devastatingly handsome he looked. "No, she must not allow herself to be attracted to such a man. He could destroy her peace. So be careful Sonia!" she said to herself.

After tea Kanwal said,"We'd better be going,"  and he opened the car door for Sonia. He was very relaxed behind the wheel. He didn't talk, and Sonia too had nothing to say. When she felt the tension mounting in her as the minutes passed in silence, she started fidgeting. Kanwal looked at her. "How long is it going to take us to reach Niel's school?" she asked.

"In another ten minutes, we'll be there."

Niel was surprised to see his mother. He had just returned to his dorm, after playing hockey, when he was told about having visitors. He became very friendly with Kanwal and wanted to go with them; but knowing the school rules Sonia said," Your uncle will come tomorrow for you. I've already requested your principal to allow you to spend the weekend with us."

On their way back, Kanwal drove in silence for a long time; his eyes on the road, his face impossible to read. This time the silence, was getting on his nerves, so he looked at Sonia and said falteringly," Sonia, when we first met in London you were different. Has life been so cruel that you've. changed totally...or is it something else?"

Sonia looked at him curiously sensing a deep interest behind the casual question. Could it be that Kanwal was more than a little interested in her past: She had never needed to explain her marriage or her past life to any one, and wasn't sure she wanted it now. "Why do you want to know? I don't like to talk about my marriage or about my life, Kanwal," she at last managed to say. "It was all in the past."

He looked disconcerted. "You must have been very young when you married Rajinder?"

"I was sixteen."

"Did you love him?" and before Sonia could answer, Kanwal shook his head." I'm prying again," he apologised. "And I've also forgotten what you asked me."

* * *

By then Sonia was lost in her past. Her father had hastily married her just to protect her from rape and abduction going on in India at the time of the political turmoil of partition of India and Pakistan, in 1947.

She hadn't met Rajinder or knew anything about him except that he was a doctor working in a London hospital. She had hated the physical union with him because he never cared whether the sexual act held any pleasure for her. He always demanded what he called his "conjugal rights."

His abuse of her gradually made it impossible for her to feel anything but loathing for any physical contact between them.

She actually despised him. Sonia recoiled from the admission.

* * *

Feeling tears falling down her cheeks, she knew she was falling apart emotionally, and if she told the truth of how she felt for her late husband, she could guess what kind of effect it would  have on Kanwal.  So meeting his  gaze with an unflinching eyes Sonia slowly said," Where does love come in arranged marriages?"

She looked frantically for a handkerchief as the tears fell in earnest.

Kanwal thought,"these words seem too cynical coming from such a beautiful woman."

He put his arm around her, "Sonia!"    she choked as she turned into him.

"So, you didn't love him. If you would rather....not talk, I can understand," he said haltingly.

"No, it doesn't matter any more." She said painfully.

Kanwal smiled. "I don't need extra sensory perception to determine that you've been badly hurt. I'd hazard it has to be your husband...though why? I knew Rajinder to be a very gentle person.

"You knew nothing about him." Sonia choked huskily.

"No?" he said meeting her tear filled gaze. Then his arm tightened convulsively, the gentleness replaced by a burning desire. He pulled her closer, stopped the car on the side of the road and gave her a light kiss while wiping her tears. He gave her no chance to explain about her husband any further, kissing her once again.

Kanwal was not flirting with her, Sonia could tell that. He found it disconcerting that she should have found such cynicism at such a young age. Her bottom lip quivered as she tried to control her tears. "I'm sorry to be so silly about this." She said between sobs. And as she turned to look at him, she realized for the first time that she loved him, loved everything about him. This revelation scared her as she didn't know how to handle her love for him. She guessed she didn't stand a chance of him feeling the same way about her. She knew from the talk she had with Radha about his attraction and engagement, with the daughter of the chief minister of a near by state. These thoughts made Sonia look at him, and the smile he gave her made her move abruptly away from him.

## CHAPTER IV

At about eight thirty when Sonia walked into the dining room she saw Kanwal talking to his mother. Her heart lurched as she gazed on his broad shoulders beneath the grey velvet jacket, and his legs fitted in black trousers. Kanwal looked at her with his face, a coolly polite mask, as he enquired what she would like to drink before dinner.

Sonia's request for a soft drink was made huskily, as her fingers dug into her upper arm with a lot of tension, for she was afraid that Radha might guess, she had fallen in love with Kanwal.

But soon her pride helped boot her courage and she walked over to him pouring the drink, determined not to let him see how he unnerved her.

Before she sat down for dinner, Ram Singh announced the arrival of Ratna. Sonia was curious as to who this visitor could be, when she saw her enter the room elegantly, in rustling silk saree with a wiff of exotic perfume. She came straight towards Kanwal lightly saying, "Isn't it wonderful, seeing you here. I thought you never wanted to come to Simla. Tell me what brought you here."

"How did you know I was here?" asked Kanwal, a bit surprised.

"I got a phone call from aunty Radha. In fact she invited me over for dinner. I thought she must have told you about it."

Sonia looked at her lovely youthful figure. Her hair was jet black; her eyes dark brown, and her complexion flawless. She was slender and had a seductive sensuous movement with her hands. Her long neck had also something sensitive about it. Sonia couldn't help looking at her dress and imagining her shapely legs beneath it, as she looked down at her high heeled sandals. It was clear that the girl had taken lot of trouble with her appearance that evening.

When Kanwal introduced her to Sonia, she felt her glance towards her a bit hostile.

Later Ratna embraced Radha before all of them sat down for dinner.

During meals Sonia saw Kanwal gazing at Ratna lovingly. She felt jealous for a while ago she had been the recipient of those soulful glances. The intimate glances Ratna was giving Kanwal made Sonia realize that she was in love with Kanwal. Anger coupled with misery coursed through her as she recalled the incident that made her aware of how much she loved him, while they were returning from Niel's school.

Ratna's sudden visit had unnerved Sonia. Her hand shook slightly as she poured herself some juice. She felt it was one thing to face a rival when you are on a secure ground, quite another when you are not aware of what the future holds for you.

Kanwal, with his head held high played the part of a perfect host. He gave every expression of being relaxed, and yet his gaze, Sonia found always mocking. Nothing had escaped his attention, not even her nervousness when she dropped her napkin, or the way her hand shook on her glass, as his gaze lingered on her.

Once when Ratna was busy talking to Radha, Sonia blushed as Kanwal'a enigmaatic gaze lingered on her.   After they returned to the drawing room, Ratna tried to have all Kanwal's attention.

"shouldn't we go now?" she prompted Kanwal. "I told Papa, I'll bring you along with me."

"Of course," saying it, he rose to his feet. Ratna took hold of his arm when she bade goodnight to Radha and Sonia. Radha looked at both of them, thinking they made an elegant couple.

With a shrug of resignation Sonia made her way to her bedroom. So much had happened, in one day, she couldn't sleep. She lay down trying to sleep, but Kanwal occupied most of her thoughts. She wanted to leave, never to see Kanwal, although she knew that the pain of loving him would not go away by her not seeing him. She questioned herself, "would she stop loving him?" Her heart naturally betrayed her. She was in a fix. She didn't know, what she should do, other than try to forget him, but she very much doubted, whether that was ever possible. She cursed herself for being mad to have fallen in love with such a man, with whom she couldn't have any future, yet that love was now a fundamental part of her. Desperately she started analyzing him.

She thought him to be a strange man, enigmatic and remote. A very deep person, with his aversion to any lasting relationship to a woman, for she wasn't stupid to realize that the passionate kisses they had shared had meant anything lasting to him. He was a man of the world and she was quite sure, he knew her very well, because under his light hearted flirting he had managaed to probe the very depth of her nature. This very thought led her to pray to God not to have him guess her feelings for him, otherwise he would simply make a mockery of her plight.

Sonia was still awake when Kanwal returned. She could hear him walk up the stairs, a door opening some distance away, and then the sound of a shower.

The thought of intimate relationship with Ratna upset Sonia and she got up from the bed. Without any conscious thought. She went down to the kitchen to make herself a cup of tea.

Hearing some one following her, she spun around almost falling over in haste. And it was embarrassing enough already without that; for she hadn't thought she would see any one, as Kanwal and his mother were in bed. Her flimsy night gown was hardly adequate clothing to be wearing in front of him. Kanwal was still in his bathrobe with the belt loosely tied; as if just out of shower.

"I couldn't sleep, so I came to make a cup of tea," Sonia said to explain her presence.

"Do you think I could?" he drawled huskily.

Sonia blushed deeply red. It was as if he had picked up the intimacy of the situation from her, his manner different from the way he had behaved earlier. She hadn't forgotton those probing glances he had given Ratna throughtout dinner.

"Sonia:" he prompted softly at her silence, "Let's have some tea." And his eyes narrowed as he looked at her.

As she saw his eyes roving on her, she folded her hands on her breast saying,"I can't. I must go, but I'll be soon back."

Mockery deepened in the tawny golden eyes when he said, "Please don't get upset for nothing," as he put two cups on the table. By then Sonia had suddenly left; but came back adequately covered by her house coat.

By then Kanwal had the tea ready. He moved to pour the tea, the mockery still in his eyes as he took in her pink robe.

In spite of the robe, Sonia felt uneasy sitting beside him, at this hour, in her night gown. She kept on telling herself, there

was nothing wrong, why feel so embarrassed, were they not both adults? With this attitude she looked at him challengingly before she picked up her cup. Kanwal sensed her attitude and couldn't help asking,
"Feeling better?"

"Yes, thank you." Still she avoided his gaze while sipping her tea. Then putting down the cup, Sonia got up, scared of the look he had been giving her; and suddenly her foot hit the leg of the table and she fell flat across the room. Kanwal quickly came to her rescue, picked her up in a second and put his arms around to steady her.

Sonia shook slightly as if she had no control over her body that was curving against him.

His mouth suddenly fused with hers and his hands moved in fevered exploration over her slender curves. Sonia could hear her heart beat a loud tattoo of uncontrolled passion. She had never known such a sensation. Her skin seemed to burn, her senses reeling from the sensuality of his probing mouth.

The moment he tried to push aside her robe, the spell was broken and the shock at her wanton behaviour made her pull back. "Please leave me alone." she choked.

Kanwal was looking at her with cool eyes when he said, "I'm sorry." And abruptly left the kitchen.

Sonia swallowed hard, realizing how easily she had succumbed to his love making. Her emotions were a confusing mixture of anger and pain. Anger because of his promise she could trust him, and pain because she had responded to him naturally for she loved him, although she knew, he was trying to take advantage of her without any feelings.

Once in bed, Sonia relived those memories of being in his arms a short while ago. She bit her lip at the thought of the man she loved. "How could I have let that happen?" she accused herself. She guessed he had been using her, perhaps teaching her a lesson. But she was quite sure that her nearness did disturb him, although these emotions had no substance in love. There relationship might be a simple attraction. If her own involvement had been more complex, that was no one's fault but her own. Certainly at no time had Kanwal led her to believe that his feelings for her were motivated by anything more than a purely physical attraction.

Sonia was vaguely aware of the time when she woke up, and with it the memory of the last night. She wondered what Kanwal would think of her. She felt reluctant to face him. Suddenly she heard voices outside her room, then the door opened and Niel came running in and hugged his mother. He looked excited when he said, "Mom, I'm going horse riding with uncle. Get ready and meet us at the band stand in an hour, as. uncle is taking us to see the Jakhoo temple."

At the band stand Sonia saw riders at a distance, and she immediately recognized Kanwal followed by Niel.
Her heart began to pound rather uncomfortably in her temples.

Kanwal was riding a black stallion followed by Niel on a mare. She instinctively appreciated the picture he presented, dressed in soft Jodhpur pants and waist coat over a fine silk shirt.

Kanwal hired a hand pulling rickshaw for his mother where as Sonia preferred to walk. Since Niel wanted to ride to Jakhoo, he followed the road taken by the rickshaw puller. Sonia and Kanwal took the pedestrian trail up the hill. At places the trail was quite steep and Sonia had to scramble up. After they had covered nearly half the distance, Sonia halted. She was breathing heavily, walking uphill. Noticing it, Kanwal held her hand tightly between his fingers before he said, "We have plenty of time to be there, just relax."

"Thank you, for the concern. I guess I can manage on my own." she said with icy politeness, before she removed her hand from his, as her pulse raced at the feel of his fingers on her hand. The hill was quite steep, and Kanwal guessed she might stumble, so he slowed down and started watching her steps. She was finding it difficult to cope with the steepness, and Kanwal was amused at her plight. Sonia was conscious about it and as she looked at him, she wondered in amazement the kind of transformation she saw in him with a smile on his face. For a second she forgot she was climbing high and her feet slipped; but a pair of hands caught at her, so strong that they seemed to lift her from the ground.

Her eyes got locked with his and time seemed to lose its beat, as their quickened breath mingled. She was virtually in his arms. For a split second her treacherous heart wanted to be there for ever; but quickly sanity returned and she got away as soon as Kanwal loosened his hold for her to move.

As they reached the top, Sonia looked around. She felt exhilarated  being there; and it lightened her heart. She appeared in a better mood as she sat down under a tree to gaze around. She found everything looked beautiful, with the sun shining warmly, and the gorse in full brightly yellow bloom, and the trees budding with the light green leaves of early spring.

A few minutes later they saw the rickshaw puller followed by the horseman holding the bridle of Niel's horse.

Soon they all reached the sacred precincts of the Hanuman mandir, the temple of the Monkey God, which stood there for centuries, still awe inspiring.

Considering it to be the home of the God, they took off their shoes and went in.

"Why are there several threads hanging around that pillar?" asked Radha.

"I was just talking to the priest about it. He told me this temple is renowned for a wish come true, so people come here to tie a thread around the pillar, and make a wish. Do you want to tie one where you find lots of them hanging?" asked Kanwal, talking to his mother while facing Sonia.

Sonia was not sure whether Kanwal was gently mocking her, but there was nothing in his looks to suggest this, so she excepted his story of the numerous wish fulfilling threads hanging by the pillar as true.

There was plenty to interest Niel among the rocky boulders, so he chattered persistently. She found him attentive to what Kanwal was explaining to him. Later Niel dragged Kanwal to the ice skating rink. Sonia and Radha stayed behind watching them, and when Niel beckoned her mother to join them she shook her head, saying, "You go ahead with Kanwal and let me watch you skating."

After the skating Sonia found Niel in high spirits and even Kanwal seemed to be infected by Niel's good humour. As they came out of the rink, Kanwal glanced at the broad gold watch on his wrist. "Let's go to The Sky Lark for a cup of tea; for there's plenty of time before I have to take back Niel to his school."

"Isn't Niel staying back for the night?" asked Sonia.

"He can't, as he has to practise for his football match."

In the grounds of the Luxury restaurant they met Ratna and her father Rai Hukam Singh. Radha folded her hands in the Indian tradition to wish him namastay. While they were talking, Ratna saw Sonia ascending the steps with Niel. She quickened her steps to be closer to them. Sonia saw Ratna and stopped to wish her. After a few pleasantries Ratna said," I understand you are leaving for Delhi tomorrow."

"I hope so," said Sonia.

"I do hope to see you on my wedding?"

Sonia managed to retain her composure. "Of course, I wish you the best of luck,"

Back to the villa, Sonia ran into the washroom and tried to wash all traces of emotion from her face, before she went for dinner and not seeing Kanwal asked Radha, "Where's Kanwal?"

"He's with the chief minister."

"You mean, Ratna's father." Sonia exclaimed incredulously.

"Yes. Her father wanted to talk to him," Radha remarked quietly." You might as well know the truth. Her father wants Kanwal to marry his daughter this fall."

Sonia didn't stay long after dinner. She pleaded headache and went back to her room. She also packed her things since they were leaving for Kanpore early morning.

It was quite late in the evening when Sonia heard Kanwal and Ratna come in, as they walked  into the courtyard, crossing her window. Once again bitter thoughts overpowered her. She was fully convinced about Ratna's motives, of seducing Kanwal at this time of the night when his mother and all the servants were all asleep. For a long time before Sonia dosed off, she kept thinking about them. Perhaps they were already lovers, and this wouldn't surprise her at all, for this beautiful girl's possessiveness seemed to stem from the experience of an intimate relationship.

At Kanpore Sonia met Narinder and his parents at Prem's residence.  She invited them to come to Delhi to meet Neena before the relationship could be finalized.  It was still early when they left for Delhi. On the way Sonia asked Radha,"Do you consider this match suitable for Neena?"

"The boy is well educated and quite handsome, and has good prospects."

"Don't you think Narinder is too much under his mother's influence?" enquired Sonia.

"Does that matter? He's already got a job abroad and will shortly be moving to Rome."

"Why don't we leave the decision to Neena?" suggested Kanwal.

"I'm really scared. I don't think they have a class," Sonia said hesitatingly.

"I'm not sure. They seem to be a good middle class family," said Radha.

"I do agree with you mother; but I can't understand why Narinder's mother is over anxious to get her son engaged to Neena?" Kanwal remarked.

"She doesn't want him to go abroad without getting married."

As customary, Neena met the whole family and for a couple of days they stayed in Delhi. Neena and Narinder went out together on a date to get to know each other. Before they left Sonia asked Neena, "Narinder's parent's want to know about our decision. Do you want to talk about it?"

"Mom, why can't you wait a little longer? How do you expect me to decide so soon. After all it's my life."

Sonia kept quiet. Neena seeing no response coming from her mother, sat down beside her and holding her mother's hand said very softly, "I know how you feel about the whole thing. I guess arranged marriages are always a gamble. I'll have to decide sooner or later. If you and Dr.Khanna feel he's compatible, I'll leave the decision to you."

After a lot of deliberation with her mother and her aunt Prem, who had in the first place suggested the match, Sonia agreed to engage Neena and Narinder. It was decided that the wedding would take place in a month's time.

Before Kanwal left for Bombay, he made arrangements for Neena to have an elaborate wedding and also left instructions with his younger brother Karan to supervise everything in his absence.

Meanwhile Sonia kept up a frantic work pace, going shopping, and ordering dresses for her daughter's trousseau; and that left little time for her to think about her own problems.

A day before the wedding Sonia went to the store room where all of Neena's trousseau as well as all the wedding gifts were put. She found an unmarked present lying on the table. Sonia opened it, to find a beautiful saree from one of Neena's friends. It should be hung with the other sarees, so she unlocked the wardrobe and pulled out a hanger. From another hanger a saree slipped and fell in a heap at her feet. Sonia recognized her own wedding dress. She suddenly noticed a faded red patch on the inside. Her heart missed a beat. She sat down on the floor with the saree on the lap. She remembered all that happened on her wedding night as if it was only yesterday. She was lost in her painful and unforgettable past.

* * *

As the train got into motion, Sonia, covered from head to foot, sat crouched on the seat. Her friend's words were ringing in her ears, " Look Sonia, you're going to be married to a man who is quite worldly and lives abroad. You are terribly inexperienced."

Sonia tried to protest but Usha her friend cut her short,

"Listen to me. You are a virgin and at sixteen you never had an opportunity of even being close to any male friend or acquaintance, as your family is quite conservative. The person you are getting married to, is a doctor nearly twice your age. Probably, he's a traditional sort of man who has agreed to marry you, without even seeing you or talking to you, just to please his parents. You're going to be travelling alone with him, the whole night, up to Delhi. He may want to make love to you; so please Sonia don't discourage him."

Suddenly she was out of her reverie when she felt some one sitting close to her. Her heart started pounding. She took it for granted, to be her husband, as they boarded a first class coupe, specially reserved for the bridal couple.

Soon she became aware of his scent, the warmth of his body and the hardness of his arms around her waist. He gradually pulled her closer to him but didn't try to lift the saree that covered her face like a veil. She was expecting him to do so any minute. To her surprise, instead, he started fumbling with her clothes. Instinctively, she caught hold of his hands. At the touch, an electric current seared her body. It was a kind of sensation she had never experienced. In spite of it she was determined to resist him. With a little force, he freed his hands and succeeded in pushing her saree from her belly. Sonia, a young bride of sixteen, tried to cover herself, but he held her hands in the grip of his left hand.

Then with the fingers of his right hand he lightly stroked her naval. Gradually he unfastened the buttons of her blouse. When he felt she was struggling hard, he forced her down, and pressed against her. She was aghast with fear.

She couldn't understand what was wrong with him. Her hands were held tightly, so she was unable to claw at him. Hastily, he put his head between the hollow of her breasts. His tongue caressed her skin in the pleasure of exploration. With one hand he cupped her breast. Sonia's body was heaving in outrage; and then suddenly a new sensation had started surging inside her when he took her, although she gasped with pain.

As the train slowed down, Sonia's partner got up hurriedly. Sonia was lying exhausted when she heard the banging of the door. She found a handkerchief lying beside her and felt something wrapped in it.

As the train ground to a halt the compartment door opened again. She heard her husband saying, "I'm glad you lay down. I was worried that you have been alone since we left Amritsar. I got down the train to fill my water bottle and the train pulled out. I just couldn't reach the compartment, so I jumped on the one behind. I,ve been sitting there for the past two hours."

* * *

While she was reminiscing she heard a knock at the door. "come in, the door is open," she called out with the saree still in her hand.

Kanwal came in. He looked at the beautiful saree that Sonia was holding, and seeing him she let it fall on the ground.

"So, you are here. I have been looking for you everywhere." With these words he came forward and picked up the saree. "What a beautiful saree! I haven't seen such a saree in the market for a long time. I don't think it is available now. From where did you get it?" he asked.

"It is one of a kind. My father had a great weaver friend, and he specially made it exclusively for me. This was the only piece. He presented it to my father, for me to wear it on my wedding. It is my bridal dress."

"There must be many more like that, for I remember having

seen one long time back; and I'm quite sure it was exactly like this. But What is it doing here with Neena's trousseau?" Kanwal said looking surprised.

"According to our family tradition, the eldest daughter has to wear her mother's bridal dress on her wedding."

"Perhaps you don't like the idea. I can see from your expression."

"You are right. It has a painful history."

"Can you change the tradition?"

"That's what I'm thinking about."

"Does Neena know about it?

"She does not."

"So don't give it to her." Kanwal said in a hoarse voice, trying to hand the saree, when suddenly the red faded patch became visible; so he looked up and there eyes met. Something inside him was bruised. With a strange restlessness, he put down the saree on the nearby table and hurriedly left saying,"I've remembered something urgent. I'll be back in the evening.

Kanwal hurried back to his car and left. He couldn't guess what happened that got him upset. He pressed down on the accelerator to pick up speed as he drove fast to be as far away as possible to be able to think clearly. He drove on for an hour, till the heat made him perspire. He rolled on the window for a breath of fresh air, before he put on the air-conditioner. He realized he had left Delhi far behind and was nearing Gurgaon, a town on the outskirts of Delhi. His senses were all raw. He suddenly remembered every word of the conversation between Rajinder and himself while playing chess, in London. The last words of Rajinder, came back to him, "I am impotent still my wife gave birth to a daughter exactly nine months after our wedding."

"Why don't you go to India and find out from your wife." Kanwal had suggested.

"You are right. I should go and confront her."

These words and Sonia's painful expression had made Kanwal feel that to help his late friend he had no choice but to find out the truth, however painful it could be; but how?

With that decision, he stopped the car near a farm and got down. He saw a farmer running the well with a camel. Kanwal went over to him. "Is this water good enough to drink?"

"Yes sir, it's cool and well chlorinated." The farmer filled a glass and handed it to him.

After Kanwal reached home, he walked restlessly around the room, trying to collect his thoughts.   It was ten minutes past eight when Kanwal drove to Sonia's house. There was music and dancing going on. Kanwal sat down quietly. Sonia noticed his disturbed looks, so she too came and sat down beside him. After a while she couldn't resist asking him, "Is something wrong? You look depressed. I guess something is bothering you."

"You are right. I can't get over the feeling that if I hadn't suggested the trip to Rajinder, he would be alive today to give his daughter's hand in marriage."

Sonia kept quiet as Kanwal continued, "I can't undo any wrong I've done to him but I have an obligation to my friend. It's my deepest desire, if you would allow me, to give away Neena as my daughter."

"Sonia looked at Kanwal in surprise. "Why do you want to go to such a length for us, Kanwal?"

"This would make me happy." Kanwal said demurely.

"I haven't given it a thought; but I certainly have no objection. After all Rajinder did make you responsible for his family. I can now guess why he had so much trust in you."

"Thank you Sonia:" Then he got up saying," Would it be all right if I left earlier?"

"The party will go on for a long time. If you want to go, you can leave earlier."

"Good night Sonia," he said gently, before he left.

Sonia watched him go. She felt miserable, and to get over her emotions, she poured herself a cup of tea.

## CHAPTER V

A huge wedding pavilion had been put up with colourful balloons in clusters, hanging from the ceiling every where. The grass was covered with a huge carpet. Sofas and chairs were arranged in rows for visitors. Strings of coloured bulbs were fastened around the outside of the pavilion, the bungalow, and the adjoining trees.

By six-thirty the guest had begun to arrive. Neena was still in her room getting dressed, with some of her doctor friends to help her.

The bride to be  was wearing a beautiful golden saree. Both her arms had a few ivory bangles embossed in red, and behind these there were twelve golden bangles. In front of these bangles there were diamond studded bracelets. Long diamond and platinum earring hung from her ears; and around her neck was a beautiful diamond necklace. On her forehead, below the centre parting, hung a golden and diamond studded pendent. This last ornament was held in place by black threads, which were fastened to her bun at the nape of her neck. On all her fingers were rings, attached with strings of pearls to a round golden medallion. The palms of her hands were decorated with henna.

Sonia and her mother had started receiving guests. Presently Kanwal arrived, immaculately dressed, with his mother on his arm and his younger brother, Karan following. All three of them carried gaily wrapped boxes. Kanwal handed his box to Tara saying, "It's a small gift for Neena."

Tara opened it to see a splendid diamond studded Tiara. "How beautiful, Kanwal. It must have cost a fortune."

"It's just a family heirloom, a gift for a daughter. It's a tradition, whenever a girl is given in marriage by the head of the family."

"Neena, is a lucky girl," said Tara.

"May I go and give this to Neena personally" Kanwal asked Sonia.

"Of course, but are you sure, you want to give her away?" Sonia sounded doubtful.

"Please, Sonia, let's not go over it again."

"Thank you very much. I can't imagine how I'm ever going to repay you for all you've done."

With the box in his hand, Kanwal went to Neena's room. At his knock, Neena opened the door. Kanwal looked at her, "You look pretty. I have a special gift to offer you. Did your mother tell you that I'll be giving you away in marriage to the lucky person, you are going to wed."

"Yes, uncle." Then looking at the tiara, "Wow, it's beautiful."

Neena's friend Dr. Kamla, was thrilled. She couldn't resist exclaiming,"In this, Neena is really going to look like a princess."

"Don't you know, she is no less than a princess?" Kanwal said with a smile.

"Uncle, would you like to adorn my head with it?"

"So you want me to crown the little princess. I would be honoured to do that ," and he laughed.  Neena too laughed. "I really feel honoured by all this.

Then she looked in the mirror and said, " Thank you uncle. I really  never expected it."

Since the wedding was to be celebrated according to the hindu  religion, the bridegroom party was supposed to reach the bride's place in a procession.  So at six in the evening, the bridegroom's party, headed by a band of thirty one musicians playing on different instruments, started from the Oberoi hotel, where Sonia had booked rooms for every one of them.

The big procession looked exactly like a fascinating parade one often watches at the Disney world. Behind the band walked the guests. Almost all the ladies were in elegant dresses, high heels, matching blouses, with pretty make up, and lot of gold and diamond jewelry. They walked beside their men folk in elegant suits, ties and highly polished boots.

In the centre of the procession one could see the bridegroom on a mare saddled with a golden saddle. He wore a long golden Achkan* and white silken pants, and a red turban on his head. Over the turban was a golden crown to which were strung jasmine flowers, that covered his face. A long sword hung at his waist. On his feet were golden leather shoes. A man walked beside the horse holding an embroidered umbrella over the bridegroom's head.  Narinder's parents walked behind him. When the procession came to a cross road, the band stopped to play tunes for the ladies and gentleman who wanted to dance, in the middle of the road. Meanwhile, the person in charge of fireworks ignited the shooting stars and fireworks to entertain the party.

* A long coat

The party slowly made through the busy streets. The band attracted women, children and men, who came out to stand on their balconies. Even passers-by stood on the side walks watching. They looked at the procession and commented among themselves, "It's a rich person's wedding." and pointed at the bridegroom who sat on the mare with the stableman leading the horse.

Occasionally Narinder's father flung a shower of small change at the bridegroom, and little urchins in the street ran to pick up the pennies. On both side of the procession, there were men in colourful uniforms carrying gas lamps to light the way and make the motorists aware of the bridal party, in order to slow down and drive carefully; as such processions were normal, in any hindu wedding. Whenever the dancers asked the band to play a special tune, they would liberally tip the leader. These tips were later on shared by all the members of the band. Behind the walking procession were rows of cars with men, women and children who preferred to ride. As soon as the procession came close to Sonia's bungalow, all the girls in their colourful, sparkling skirts and blouses ran to the upper storey to watch from the windows or the balconies.

According to the time old custom, Neena was asked to stand on the balcony with her friends, to see her bridegroom coming to wed her on a horseback. The band stood playing at the gate. By then Kanwal along with Sonia and Tara, stood welcoming the bridegroom's party. Photographers were busy taking shots. Neena followed by her friends came to the front door with a garland of flowers. The bridegroom too got down the horse and stood facing Neena . He too had a garland in his hand. With the chanting of the mantras by the priest, the bridegroom put the garland around Neena's neck.

Then she too put the garland around Narinder's neck. This was a gesture that showed all the friends and relatives gathered that the bride and the groom were willing to get married without any pressure from any one.

As soon as this rite was completed, the party came in and sat down. Waiters from the Sheraton hotel, in white uniforms, began serving the guests, cold drinks, tea, coffee and various snacks. The guests relished them and sat enjoying the songs sung by artists. There was much clapping and laughter. Then dinner was announced. The guest filled their plates from tables that looked exotic with every sort of delicacy, laid in fine china and silver bowls. After the dinner all the guests settled down to watch the wedding.

The bride and the bridegroom were taken to the alter, and asked to sit on special cushioned seats. Sonia and Kanwal sat crossed legs on the rug on Neena's side, and Narinder's parents sat opposite, near their son. In front of the bridegroom was an iron cauldron, filled with strips of mango-tree bark. And beside these, one could see melted butter and samigri* in silver plates. Opposite the bride and the groom sat the priest on a two square feet carpet. The priest chanted mantras from the scriptures , and asked the groom to light the fire in the cauldron. Once the fire was lighted, and a few preliminary mantras sung, the priest asked Sonia who was going to give away the bride. Kanwal stood up. He held Neena's hand while he repeated the mantras after the priest, and then put her hand in Narinder's hand. The bride and the bridegroom were then told to encircle the fire in the cauldron four times. Later the groom was handed a red powder which, with the chanting of the mantras, he put it slowly in the centre parting of the bride's hair. In the end the

* Mixture of grounded herbs

groom repeated mantras after the priest that meant, "I wed Neena with this solemn oath, to look after her, be loyal to her till the end of my life."

Neena too repeated the mantras after the priest saying,"I wed Narinder with the solemn oath to be faithful to him, and to be loyal to him till the end of my life."

Then the bride and the groom took seven small steps to confirm their solemn oath and the priest announced them as husband and wife.

There were tears in Neena's eyes when she boarded the train for Kanpore. Kanwal hugged Neena and two tears glided down his cheeks. Brushing them away, he said, "Take care of your self. Don't ever hesitate to write to me if you have any problem."

"Thank you uncle. Please, take care of Mom. Don't let her feel lonely."

As the train moved off, tears streamed down Sonia's cheeks, blurring her vision. Hesitatingly, Kanwal put his arm around her, "Sonia, please try to calm down. Neena had to go to her home, that's life. Can you not count on me as your friend who'll always be here, whenever you need me?"

Sonia liked the way Kanwal held her close. She could feel the wealth of tenderness that emanated from his actions and his words. "Did he really mean he would always seek her out no matter how far she strayed from him? On a second thought, what when he gets married?" She questioned herself. He then held her arm and in silence escorted her to the car. When they had been driving for a few minutes, he said, "You've been busy preparing Neena's trousseau all these months, but now you are free, and your mother too is going back to Amritsar; have you any plans of what you'll be doing to keep yourself occupied?"

Sonia didn't reply. Kanwal put his hand on hers and again spoke very tenderly, "I do hope you'll try to take hold of yourself. Perhaps it would be better if we talk about this and other things tomorrow."

When Kanwal helped Sonia get out of the car,  her legs were still shaky.   She sat down on the sofa in the living room , as soon as she entered the room. Kanwal too sat down beside her. With a very assuring smile he said, "I've asked Gopal to get something for you to drink. As soon as he brings the drink I'll be on my way."

"Of course, it has been a long day. Thank you very much. " Then in a shrill voice full of emotion, Sonia looked at Kanwal and said, "Kanwal, you have already done a lot for the family. In future, you've no need to take your responsibility for us so heavily. I'm sure Rajinder didn't intend......"

Before she could say any thing else, Kanwal took her hand . As their hands touched, both of them felt a jolt of a strong sensation sear through their bodies, but with a thumping heart, Kanwal managed to look into her eyes and said, "Rajinder made his intentions perfectly clear. I don't find it so onerous, you know. I wish I could serve you with all my heart and soul, if only you'd allow me to."

To get over the situation, Sonia hurriedly said, "It's all right, Kanwal. I know how you feel."

Kanwal stood up. Sonia had a dreadful feeling that she had over stepped the bounds of politeness. "I'm sorry. I never meant to be rude." Tears glistened in her eyes.

Kanwal too lost control of himself for a moment. He put his arm around her and tried to console her. "It wasn't my fault," she sobbed brokenly, her fingers convulsively clutching and un-clutching his hand, I ......coul.d .n.... 't he....l..p..........i..t"

Kanwal led her tenderly, to the door of her bedroom. "Now go to sleep. I'll see you in the morning."

Tripta helped Sonia change and comb her hair. She brought her a glass of warm milk. Sonia got into her bed. She tried to dispel the warning voices that kept whispering to her. She couldn't stop thinking of Kanwal, remembering how she tried to get away from him.

She moaned softly as her mind kept reliving the past two weeks. Restlessly she thumped her pillow. Then turning on her side and gazing at her daughter's picture on the night table she, at last, fell asleep.

In the morning, as she showered and dressed, the situation didn't seem quite so threatening. She went to the shrine, to pray. Sonia knelt down before the idol of Lord Krishna and Radha, and lit all the candles as well as the perfumed incense sticks. However hard she tried to focus her attention to Lord Krishna's image, her thoughts kept drifting towards Kanwal. Last night while he was holding her, she thought he looked much younger, free of care, happy and likeable. With these thoughts distracting her, Sonia couldn't pray. She therefore asked forgiveness from the Lord and left the shrine, and went to the kitchen to prepare a cup of tea. Inadvertently, she muttered to her self, "I just don't want to get hurt again,"

She was quite sure, there could be no future for her with Kanwal. So she decided to harden herself against all thoughts of him. She wouldn't let his image disrupt her as it had for the last months since Kanwal came to India.

Sonia was out of her reverie as she heard the clinking of plates in the dining room where Nand was laying the table. She stood up to go and see her mother, when she heard the phone ring. It was Neena at the other end.

"When did you reach Kanpore? Are you okay? How was

the journey?" she asked excitedly in one breath. "Mom, I"m fine. We got here early this morning. Since then I've been trying to get through to you, but the line was busy." then added, "I know you were worried about us travelling by train. I assure you nothing untoward happened."

Sonia could hear her daughter's laughter when she said, "We didn't encounter any dacoits on the way. Does that make you feel better?"

Later Sonia and Tara entered the dining room where breakfast had been laid. "Mother how long do you intend to stay at Amritsar?" asked Sonia.

"Most probably I'll be back by Diwali*

"I keep worrying about you. You're not in the best of health, and I don't want you to be on your own."

They were still talking when the door bell rang. Gopal answered the door. Tara stood up saying, "I'd better go to my room and finish packing. May be that's Kanwal already here to give me a ride to the station."

A loud thunderclap made Sonia look towards the window, where large rain drops were now tapping on the window panes. She cautioned her mother. "It's raining. Don't forget to keep your rain coat and umbrella handy."

"I will. I know it won't last long, as the wind is blowing hard. It's likely the clouds will soon disperse."

When Gopal opened the front door, Sonia saw Kanwal standing on the porch, with raindrops sparkling on the light brown hair. She greeted him casually. Kanwal too wished her well, and without further talking to her, went straight to her mother's room, and knocked before he said, "Are you ready, Mrs. Dhingra?" Tara opened the door and greeted Kanwal. "Yes, in another ten minutes. Would you mind

* Festival of lights

waiting for me in the drawing room?"

Kanwal entered the drawing room and stared at the drizzling rain. Sonia followed him. "Will you have something to drink?" she asked softly.

Kanwal lost in thoughts, didn't hear her. Something in Kanwal's behaviour puzzled her. She tried again. He turned around hearing her footsteps. "Did you say something?" he asked.  In stead, she said, "I had a phone call from Neena an hour ago. She asked me to thank you."

"Did she sound happy?"

Before she could say anything more, Tara came out with her bags. Kanwal took them and led her to his car. Having settled her in, he turned , looked briefly back at Sonia, then got in and drove off.

Sonia watched him from the window until his form disappeared. The thought of his getting married to Ratna was like a shaft through her chest. Not able to bear the blow, she went forward to open the window and let the fresh air blow on her face, as to cool the fever in her mind. After a while with a deep breath she said to herself, "you little fool, I know how you feel."

For the next two days, Sonia did not see Kanwal. Then he phoned to find out if she would be home that afternoon. Before Sonia put down the receiver she couldn't help saying, "since you are coming over, have lunch here." and without waiting for his reply, she put down the receiver, and was mad at her own behaviour. How ever hard she was trying to make up her mind to get over her feelings for him, she seized every chance to be close to him though  quite aware of the consequences.  Her heart was still beating fast just to hear his voice on the telephone.

Sonia was  impatiently waiting for his arrival. When at last the bell rang, she jumped up, but Tripta who was closer to the door said, I'll get it." She saw Kanwal immaculately dressed for the city in a grey pin-stripe suit. The open jacket revealed the matching waist coat beneath and the trousers moulded the powerful muscles of his thighs.

As usual Sonia was thrown off balance as he looked back at her and gave a broad smile which deepened the grooves around his mouth. Tripta folded her hands to wish him and said, "Namastay, sir, do come in."

Kanwal greeted Sonia and sat beside her on the couch. For a few minutes no one spoke. "On the phone, you seemed to have an urgency to come and see me. Is something wrong with the Will?"

Slowly Kanwal put his arm along the back of the couch and said, "Pleas don't misinterpret. I've come to you with a request. It's about my mother,"

"What is it?" Sonia was apprehensive.

"Lately my mother has not been feeling well. I had her examined thoroughly. The tests show she might be suffering from leukaemia. I have to take her to the Bombay cancer hospital immediately." For a few seconds he didn't say anything and then added very slowly, "My younger brother Karan is busy with his studies. He's to get his doctor's degree in six months. I don't want to upset him. So I've come to you. Can you go with us? It would be a great relief for me and my mother if we have you with us. I hope I'm not asking too much."

"I'm glad you came to me. Surely, I would like to accompany you to Bombay." Sonia said unhesitatingly. "I'll try my best."

"I hope I"m not imposing on you?" Kanwal's arm left the back of the sofa and settled around her shoulders. Sonia didn't flinch. Perhaps she wanted his arm there.

Gopal announced that lunch had been served. After his coffee, Kanwal looked at his wrist watch and said, "I'm going to book our seats for the morning flight. Please bring Tripta with you."

In the evening Sonia contacted Neena on the phone and gave her the news. Then she started packing her bags.


## CHAPTER VI


Their flight to Bombay was very smooth. As soon as the plane landed at the Santa Cruz air port, Kanwal saw his driver Rahul waiting for them in the lounge. Hel personally pushed his mother's wheel chair up to the car. Then having made Radha comfortable he helped Sonia in. It was a long drive from the airport to Bombay City. At many places they had to slow down because of rush hour traffic. Their car slowly edged its way through the busy roads until it crossed Grant Road Station.

From their onward to Marine drive was a smooth and fast journey. As the speed increased Sonia looked at the vast expanse of the blue sky on one side of the road and the huge multi storey buildings on the other. These aristocratic mansions were most colourful, with gardens and lawns on all sides. Even the encircling walls had wide parapets on which she saw different kinds of pots with all sorts of flowers blooming. In front of some of the modern bungalows there were small marble statues, or miniature fountains from which water sprayed in graceful arcs.

The car slowed down outside a huge iron gate which was

immediately opened by a liveried servant. They drove in and halted by the porch. The manager Mr. Om Parkash, welcomed them. While Ram Singh the butler, was arranging the wheel chair, Sonia was astonished to read the name of the bungalow,"THE BRIDE" written in bold letters.

Kanwal helped his mother get into the wheel chair. She wanted to walk but he insisted she should use the chair and not tire herself.

Sonia saw the huge oak double door wide open, and all the servants standing in a line to wish them welcome. Each and every servant touched Radha's feet, before they bowed down to their master. They also greeted Sonia with folded hands.

As soon as they stepped in, Sonia found herself in a very big stone hall inlaid with marble. It was palatial with spiral stairs on all the corners; and a gallery three feet wide running around the length and breadth of the hall. As she looked up Sonia saw numerous arched doorways open, giving glimpses of rooms on the upper floor. The hall was decorated with woven tapestry here and there, and potteries in brilliant shades and designs hanging from the gallery ceilings. All the couches and chairs were of either sheep or goat skin leather or deep red velvet, and white rugs with colourful designs covered the marble floor.

Kanwal took his mother's wheel chair to the west wing of the bungalow and halted before a huge double door. Ram Singh turned the handle and opened it. Sonia who too was walking beside them found Radha's bedroom, very elegant and it even surpassed his house in Delhi.

After instructions to his mother's personal maid Kulwant to massage her feet to make her relax and go to sleep, he turned his attention to Sonia.    "You too look tired. Come, I'll show you to your room."

Sonia and Tripta followed Kanwal. They went up a few steps to a slightly higher level. Kanwal opened the first door to the right.

Sonia saw a spacious room with a wide expanse of soft carpet on the marble floor. In the centre was a huge four poster bed with silken covers. There were also television and hi-fi-equipment with the fitted units. Like the hall, the room had goat skin couches covered with attractively embroidered cushions. There was a massive double wardrobe and a dressing table with carved legs.

The long french windows stood wide open and through them came a soft fragrance from the garden below. Long, wide silk curtains in a delicious shade of green moved slightly with the breeze. Outside, Sonia could see the wide expanse of the sea, and the waves that foamed as they curled along the rock-strewn beach. Kanwal opened two more doors to show her the attached bathroom and the dressing room. He left her with a smile, saying, "Dinner will be at eight."

Sonia threw her bag on the bed and stood near the window to look at the vast expanse of the sea. She could feel the trickle of sweat at the nape of her neck. Her forehead and palms were also damp. It was very hot and humid, so she decided to have a bath.

Like the rest of the bungalow the bath room too was commodious and tiled in turquoise. It had a separate shower unit in addition to the marble sunken bath. The glass shelves above the vast circular bath were filled with bottles of bath essence and body lotions, boxes of talcum and dusting powders and all manners of fragrance intended to make bathing a more delightful experience. Sonia stayed a long time in the tub. When at last she came out and lay down for her siesta she felt cool and relaxed. Soon she went to sleep.

When Sonia woke up, the sun was dipping behind the vast expanse of the sea, shedding its orange glow. By then dozens of insects were visible in the light that streamed from windows back along the villa.

Soon she dressed herself in a blue muslin saree with a matching blouse and petticoat, and a pair of Kholapuri* chappals* on her feet. It was nearly eight o'clock when she came out of her room.

Kanwal was waiting for her on the terrace outside. He too looked coolly relaxed in cream silk pants and a dark blue silk shirt which was open at the throat to reveal his gold chain with a tiny gold medallion suspended from it.

Kanwal put his hand over hers, holding it against his arm, while getting her down the flight of steps. Her pulses raced alarmingly at this gesture, although she gave in reluctantly but not without some misgivings.

It seemed to her that Kanwal was taking her on a tour of the place. In his proximity, Sonia's thoughts always got confused. Suddenly her love for him surged through her, and she felt jealous of Ratna. But soon she realized she was foolish to fall in love with him; because the moment he gets married, she would be relegated to her true position in his life.

Sonia was out of her reverie as soon as they reached the informal dining area, when she heard Kanwal telling her about it and about the actual dining hall beyond it, with a long table capable of seating more than a dozen people. She also glanced at the kitchen which too contained eating facilities, and was in fact sleek and modern.

The lounge had long windows with slatted blinds. It had soft velvet couches in shade of blue and green,

* A city in India.  * Shoes

modern furniture cheek by jowl with obvious antiques and silky off white carpeting.

After the tour Kanwal brought back Sonia once again to the dining room.  By then the table had been laid. She couldn't help admiring the finely woven lace mats and the shining silver and crystal.

"Please have a seat," Kanwal said politely as he pulled a chair for her.  He then moved away from her to a tray of drinks placed on a low carved table. "What would you like to drink?"

"I'm not thirsty," she said, looking at the wall cabinet which revealed a collection of wood carvings, which strangely seemed alien to the environment.

"Surely, do drink something. It's quite hot. something cold will refresh you."

"very well, I'd prefer some fruit juice, if you don't  mind."

As soon as they settled down, Sonia felt that in these lamplight surroundings his darkness was accentuated by the room's white walls. Kanwal too had noticed the tautness of Sonia's body, the stiff way she held herself, as if she was afraid of something and so unable to relax.

The table was set for two. Sonia sat on Kanwal's right hand. Chikku the bearer was handing dishes.

"You are hardly eating anything."

"I'm not  hungry."

"Is something worrying you? since we started from Delhi, I haven't seen you relax. You must take care of yourself." He said  looking concerned. His eyes had a caressing quality which weakened her knees and set her trembling.

Kanwal kept handing her the dishes, and reluctantly she had to fill her plate. She kept her eyes on her plate because she didn't have the courage to look at him, scared of betraying her feelings.

The ease and familiarity with which Kanwal began talking to her made her eventually relax. "How is your mother now?" Sonia asked and to keep up the conversation she added, "I wanted to go and see her but I was'nt sure she would want to be disturbed."

"She feels weak. I was with her earlier and took her for a stroll in the garden. She loves to see the flowers blooming around."

"Is she going to be admitted to the hospital, right away?"

"I'm afraid she has to, although she doesn't like the idea; but it can't be helped."

"Would you like me to come with you when you take her there?"

"There would be many formalities to undergo. Wouldn't it be better if you accompanied me in the evening, after she's admitted?"

With dinner over, Kanwal and Sonia sat on the couch. Coffee was served to them. After coffee, Kanwal said,
" How about a stroll in the garden?"

Sonia was reluctant. She knew he belonged to Ratna; and was just being civil to her. But when Kanwal persuaded her, she yielded, drawn by the lure of being in his company a little longer. They stepped out on the lawn through the french windows, and looked across at the shadowy garden, smelling the night scented blossoms and hearing the murmur of the sea at the distance. For sometimes they strolled leisurely till they came upon a seat in a perfumed arbour. Sonia leaned back against the hard branches from which the rustic seat had been fashioned. Kanwal left her there to relax and strolled on a little ahead deep in thought.

The air was soft and sweet. The vast vault of the night sky, looked like a compound of moonlight and starlight, deep purple velvet, that had a soothing effect. The garden, bathed in silver effulgence and encompassed in silence, and lulled by the gentle music of the fountain made Sonia very drowsy.

She rose unsteadily as Kanwal reappeared at the entrance to the secluded arbour. Suddenly the luminous reflection of the moon fell on the ornamental fountain in the distance. The simple harmonious tones of light and shade, where the bulbs were sparkling off and on, attracted Sonia.

"That fountain looks breath takingly wonderful."

"Shall we walk over there by the fountain?" He said a little reluctantly.

It was slightly cooler near the fountain, and the breeze of the falling water was refreshing. To her amazement, she saw a marble figure of a half naked woman with a veil carved to represent finest lace. Through the beautiful carving, studded with small coloured bulbs that twinkled off and on, she saw a shy, smiling lips of the statue. From the two nipples of the breasts water gushed, looking in the reflection of the silky white bulbs that played on it, like two streams of milk. The lively fountain sent forth myriad rainbows to add enchantment and romance to the fairy tale scene. Under the statue's right breast was a black mole that enhanced its beauty. The artist must have put it there to protect the human form in marble from the evil eye. It was indeed a superb sculpture.

As Sonia caught sight of that black mole, her breath got caught in her throat and she staggered. For a moment she was lost in her painful past. She felt as if the stranger was exciting her nerves by licking the mole. How often she had longed for that sensation, but she never had it while sleeping with her husband. She came out of her reverie as Kanwal asked, "Is something wrong?"

Sonia couldn't answer. She felt the hot colour burn her cheeks. She leaned against the tree for support, seeing this Kanwal caught her shoulders, and she felt herself pulled against his chest. Soon she clasped his waist to keep herself from falling. Kanwal lifted her clear off the ground and held her closer still. Sonia clung to him with a passion that left her breathless.

"Are you all right? Would you like to tell me, what happened?"

How could she tell him what the sculpture reminded her of. Instead, she said, "I remembered something from my past."

"The past is dead. If I were you, I would never give it a second thought. Only the present and the future are important." He said very sincerely while laying her down on the marble seat, a few yards away from the fountain, and still keeping his arms around her, when he sat down beside her.

She didn't dare open her eyes. Her heart was thudding at his nearness. When she finally looked at him, Kanwal saw in the nearby lamp light the unshed tears glistening behind her eyes. He shook his head compassionately, before he spoke soothingly, "Listen to me. Once the past is forgotten, I assure you, your life will have a new charm and you'll enjoy it."

Sonia had tried several times to forget her past. Unfortunately something kept coming up to revive it. She felt that fate was too powerful, and she couldn't fight her destiny.

Kanwal put his hand on her forehead and caressing it asked very softly, " Will you promise to forget the past?"

Sonia's heart refused to slow down, and as her lips seemed frozen, she couldn't speak. It was difficult for Kanwal to see her suffering, but he had no other choice but to keep quiet.

After a while Sonia sat up, and turned her head away, not

that it helped very much when she was already in his arms. At the same time she couldn't help thinking, "Why does he care so much for me when he owes his allegiance to another woman?" The thought brought a flash of anger, then she remembered that she was here as his guest, to help his mother, who had always been kind to her, as Kanwal himself had been. How could she forget all he had done for her and her children?

She guessed the present situation was just circumstantial. He had always behaved like a gentleman. She could feel only friendly concern in his touch, and so with a sigh she relaxed against him, resting her head on his shoulders. At last she looked up at him, "Kanwal, how can I thank you enough for giving me so much courage? But when you won't be around, how will I be able to face the world?"

"Don't worry. I'll always be near you, to protect you. Rajinder trusted me and left you in my care. You all are a part of my family. Remember, this is very important." Then he cupped her face in his hands and kissed her very lightly on the forehead, before he spoke again, "Let's go in. We need a strong cup of coffee to settle our nerves."

Kanwal took her hand and led her inside. She went into her bedroom. After a while the door opened, and in came Kanwal with two cups of steaming coffee on a tray. He put it on the table in front of her and sat down.

"Why did you bother? Tripta could have brought the coffee?"

"I like to serve my near and dear ones personally."
When Sonia looked at him, he hastily added, this is just an excuse, "I really needed company. Besides, I'm a doctor, and I wanted to know how you feel now."

They sipped their coffee and when both got up, he gave

Sonia a hug which was as impersonal as possible. Before he left he said, "Have a nice sleep, and bury the past.

Sonia got up early as usual, in spite of the events of last night, she had a dreamless sleep. After bath and her morning prayers, she stood near the open window of her room. It was a beautiful morning, the air delicately fresh and cool. The sky was the palest blue, shading to turquoise as sea and sky melted into each other.

All of a sudden she remembered Kanwal telling her to come down for breakfast at eight thirty, as a little later he would be taking his mother to the hospital. Sonia wanted to see her off, so she hurried out.

The door of Kanwal's room was ajar. Sonia saw him leaning against the wardrobe. He glanced at her with cool appraising eyes and said, "Come in Sonia."

Though Kanwal was fully dressed, yet Sonia was reluctant to enter. She paused on the threshold before she stepped in. She looked around. It was a spacious room, designed in shades of coffee and cream, with thick apricot satin curtains at the window.

"The doctor phoned a change of time as he's busy in the morning. Since we'll be leaving at eleven thirty, would you like to come with us?"

"Of course, if it's convenient." She said enthusiastically.

"Let's go and have breakfast."

Radha was sitting in the wheel chair when Sonia entered followed by Kanwal. Breakfast was served in the small elegant room overlooking the court yard, with the fountain spraying over the garden. Sonia wished Radha before she asked, "How are you feeling today?"

"I'm fine. thank you."

Sonia sat down on the couch and talked to Radha, while

Kanwal stood watching them. After a while he looked at his wrist watch and said, "It's time for us to leave."

At the hospital Kanwal met Dr. Parikh in the lobby. Radha was taken to her room by a nurse with Sonia following her, while Kanwal stood talking to the doctor.

"I've already gone through the results you sent me of her tests. I fully agree that the proliferation of leucocytes is there; but unless we take more tests here, I can't be sure. It will take a couple of days to do all of them. After that, if the results are the same, I'd like to give her a complete blood transfusion to increase the level of blood haemoglobin to counteract the effect of anaemia."

"In Delhi, the doctors felt there was also a slight enlargement of the spleen," said Kanwal.

"If I find that, I'll immediately start the steroid hormone medication, to reduce it. Please don't worry, Khanna. I'll do my best for her. I've also contacted Dr.Vincent Smith, in New York, as promised. He's an authority on this and has cured a couple of cases. If the worst comes to worst, we could give her the bone marrow transfusion. By the time we get confirmation from New York, she'll be better able to take the journey."

After the nurse left Radha and Sonia in the room, Radha said, "Sonia, did you ask Kanwal my question?"

"Don't worry about it. Just get well. I'm sure he'll keep his word, but this is no time for these things to be discussed."

"I'm convinced I can't be cured of this disease. Before I die, I want him to get married. Please tell him, Ratna's father phoned me last night again. He wants me to confirm the engagement."

While they were talking, Kanwal and Dr.Parikh came in.

"How long do you want to keep me in the hospital?" asked

Radha.   "We'll send you home as soon as possible."

"Take care mother, we'll be with you in the evening."

Radha was feeling very weak. As soon as she closed her eyes Kanwal and Sonia left.  Kanwal was depressed. He drove back silently.

On the morning of the third day, Radha was given complete blood transfusion. She was not allowed any visitors for another couple of days. On the fifth day Kanwal and Sonia visited her. She looked rested and much better. Kanwal also met Dr.Parikh who said, "The spleen is returning to normal. We have great hope of curing her, but this could just be a temporary phase. I would like to watch her symptoms for another week and then allow her to go home."

The next morning Kanwal came to Sonia's room and said, "I'm going out. After I finish my work, I'll visit mother and return by noon. If I were you, I'd go out for a walk on the sea beach. It's a nice cool day."

After Kanwal left, Sonia opened the french door and stepped out on the paved patio. She saw two gardeners at work. She stopped to speak to one who was sweeping dead leaves from the lawn. A few minutes later she went and sat down in the shade of the fruit trees, close to the fountain which was spraying water all around. The musical sound lulled her and she dozed off until Tripta came to accompany her to the beach.

Hearing footsteps, Sonia woke up, still filled with delight at her surroundings. Followed by her maid, she went towards the tall coconut trees. On the left where the land rose higher, covered with small bushes, she saw a goat tethered to a tree. Perhaps Sonia wanted to be a part of this general tranquillity. Subconsciously, she was seeking among those trees rest, from the thoughts that still frightened her.

To her right she could see the wide expanse of the sea. It looked warm and inviting even to a non-swimmer like herself. She crossed the small patio and reached the sun kissed beach that was broken some distance away by a few jutting rocks behind which she could see Kanwal's private boat house. Kicking off her sandals, she walked to the water's edge and allowed the tiny waves to curl around her toes. The water was like silk and warm, and grain of sand tickled her feet. She bent down to roll back the cuffs of her pants and almost jumped out of her skin when she heard Kanwal's voice saying, "Hello, Sonia! Enjoying yourself?"

Jerking upright she swung around, to find him standing a few yards away, his only garment a pair of shorts that left bare the hairy expanse of the chest and his long powerful legs.

Sonia's eyes travelled over the hard muscular length of his body. "The sea is really warm and soft. I thought I would wade along the shore."

"How about a swim?"

"You know I can't swim."

"I'm supposed to be a good teacher. Try me again. Let Tripta get your swim suit."

Sonia had missed his company for the last week. She acquiesced and sent the maid for the things.

Sonia had to admit to herself that his nearness always exhilarated her. She stared at him with a mixture of pain and compassion. Her swimsuit came and she went behind the rocks to change.

When she came out Kanwal glanced at her with a cool appraising eye, then took her hand and led her into the water to her waist. The sea gleamed invitingly. Kanwal didn't speak, just held her hand and she felt happy.

"How about giving you a second lesson?" he said. Then putting his hands on her shoulders, added, "Take a deep breath and get your head under the water."

At his masterful touch, she forced her head under, letting the wave break over it a moment before she came up. Kanwal came closer. Curving his hand under her chin, raised it to inspect her face.

Sonia was happy at her achievement. She felt contented just to gaze at his compelling masculinity. Kanwal grinned at her, "Want to do it again?"

Sonia nodded and repeated the experience. Slowly she started swimming. Kanwal swam closer and said, "You are doing fine. I know you can swim but you lack confidence." While he was talking, a strong wave came from nowhere and she was pushed against him. Involuntarily Kanwal's arms went around her. The closeness of her body was rapidly banishing all other thoughts from her head. She could feel the muscled strength of his limbs against hers, and her weakness made her yield involuntarily so she looked up invitingly and he automatically bent down to meet her lips. The kiss was hard and hungry, demanding a response and gaining it from her lips. The sensuality of their embrace was heightened every minute she was pressed against him. His tongue against her sensitized skin ignited her emotions, so she couldn't tell him to let her go. But before she could react, Kanwal thrust her determinedly away from him. "I'm sorry. This was not my intention," he muttered huskily.

Sonia looked at Kanwal uncomprehendingly. Her excitement was evident. She found his attention focused on her, and Kanwal stepped back releasing her head and removing his other hand from her waist. "We should go back," he said, his jaw clenched tautly.

Sonia endeavoured to recover a sense of proportion, desperately anxious that Kanwal should not be aware of her love for him. By now Sonia was quite sure Kanwal's intentions were honourable. He wasn't taking advantage of the situation, he merely had tried to teach her to be a perfect swimmer.

They ate their lunch in the lounge, where a folding table sent up from the dining area had been set up by the window, with its panoramic view of the sea and the rocks on which the waves curled in foamy spray.

With lunch over Sonia went to her room and lay down to sleep. When she woke up, it was evening. She felt someone's presence in the room, and saw Kanwal standing by the window. At the sound of movement behind him, he too turned. "So you're awake." His appraisal was without feeling. It's tea time. Won't you keep company?" Sonia didn't have the breath to answer him, but simply followed him out.

Kanwal too was silent and she was glad. They drank their tea and relished samosas*. While they were still sitting with their cups, the phone rang.

It was Neena's voice at the other end. Kanwal handed it to Sonia. After putting down the receiver, Sonia told Kanwal, "Neena and Narinder are coming to Bombay, back from their honeymoon, tomorrow morning by Indian Airline. Can we go to receive them?"

"Sure. At what time is the flight coming in?"

"At eight thirty in the morning."

Sonia and Kanwal sat talking and discussing small events, and then Sonia went to her room to change for dinner.

A little before eight Kanwal received a long distance call from Simla. He took the call in the drawing room. He was

* A kind of pie filled with potatoes

speaking a little loudly due to bad connection. "Hello, Ratna, so nice to hear your voice."

"Mother is feeling better but in a fortnight I'm taking her to New York as I don't want to take any chance. I want the best medical aid for her." Then he asked, "When are you completing your internship at the Snow Down hospital at Simla?"

"Yes, I do remember you want to get a job in The States...."

While he was still talking to her, Sonia came down to join Kanwal for dinner. She heard Kanwal say, "Don't worry, Ratna. There could be a little delay because of the unforseen circumstances, but I'll keep my promise."

Sonia moved away restlessly to stand by the tall windows of her room that faced the sea beach. She was upset because of what she heard Kanwal say to Ratna on the phone. The words were still ringing in her ears. Her throat got constricted. What stupid impulse had brought her to Bombay? Why had she succumbed to his charm and brought such an emotional catastrophe in her life. She had been happy, had made a life for her in India after she left her husband. Now, through this crazy impulse, she had lost her peace of mind.

Sonia was thus lost in her thoughts when Kanwal came looking for her. "what are you doing here in the dark? what's bothering you?" he asked as he stood close to her.

"Nothing is bothering me," she insisted in cool dismissal.

"Something is," he persisted, holding her hand. Then he added, "Why didn't you come down for dinner?"

When Sonia turned towards him, she could see his grim features. She felt nervous, and couldn't look straight at him, afraid of revealing feelings of love that her expressive eyes might reveal.

I know you must have been again lost in your past, and so forgot all about dinner."

Sonia felt a little better when she realized that Kanwal had misjudged the cause. "I'm sorry, it's true I lost count of the time."

"Now lets go and eat something." She followed Kanwal to the dinning room. After they sat down, Kanwal studied her more closely to discover what had suddenly gone wrong, for he found her in a kind of tension. Sonia ate very little. Kanwal tried to talk her out of this tension, but she managed only a stiff nod or stilted reply when he addressed her. Her head buzzed. She wanted to leave the table, but her good manners kept her from leaving.

After dinner they sat in the drawing room with cups of coffee. To cheer her up Kanwal put on the automatic player and music filled the room. This was the first time he showed interest in music. Then he turned to her and asked, "Do you recognize the music, we danced to, in London at the hospital party?"

Sonia just nodded. Kanwal stood up and touched Sonia's arm, "How about a dance?"

"I'm tired. I'd like to go to my room and get some rest." She looked at Kanwal. Pride kept her head high while a defensiveness masked her gaze with a wary coolness.

Kanwal made no attempt to touch her as they walked. Quietly they mounted the exquisitely curved staircase, whose balustrade was gilded wrought iron in an intricate design. The upper landing was wide, and thickly carpeted; so it made no sound as they both walked. Kanwal held the door open for her to enter and before he left, he said very softly, "Goodnight, Sonia, sleep well."

Sonia undressed and slipped on her night dress. Switching

off the light, she crawled under the covers of her bed. She guessed how jealous she could be and how easily hurt. She suggested to herself that such an intensity wasn't good for her and promised once she is away from him, she will see that it naturally burns itself out. She knew she had only to wait, because she couldn't leave immediately as she had promised to be there to help him during his mother's sickness.

She couldn't sleep for a long time. She could hear the sound of the surf as it beat on the rocky surface. To get out of her emotional crisis, she slid out of bed and walked on her balcony to breathe the tangy sea breeze. After a while she lay down. In spite of her emotional crises, the magic air soothed her nerves and she later went into a dreamless sleep.

The next morning Sonia was delighted to meet Neena and Narinder when they alighted from the plane. Kanwal too shook hands with Narinder and hugged Neena.

At the hospital Neena talked to Radha. After the visiting hours, as Neena stepped out of the room, she saw Dr.Mohan coming towards her, "Hi, Neena, what a surprise?" Mohan said.

"Hello, Mohan, I never expected to see you here. Do you work here?"    "My mother is a patient here. She had breast cancer. She has been operated. Thank God, she is now out of danger."

Later, Neena introduced Narinder, Kanwal and Sonia to him. "What are you doing here?" he asked.

"I came to visit Dr.Khanna's mother who's suffering from blood cancer."

"What a strange coincidence?" he said. "I was planning to go and see you at Delhi. I never dreamt you had got married."

"Didn't you get my invitation card?"

During the next few days Sonia enjoyed sight seeing with

Neena and Narinder. On the eve of their departure Neena said, "Mom, we are leaving for Rome within a fortnight. On our way we want to go to London and Paris. Can I have some foreign money to spend?"

"How much do you need?"

"How about a thousand pounds?"

"Have you talked to Kanwal? You know we can't spend even a penny without his consent."

"Mom, why don't you talk to him?"

"Very well tonight I'll go and speak to him."

After Neena and Narinder went out for a late show, Sonia knocked at Kanwal's bedroom. He opened the door, and said, "Do come in."

Sonia sat on the couch a little hesitant. She scuffed her bare toe against a skin rug before she explained why Neena wanted some foreign money.

"Neena is an heiress. Whatever she likes, she can have. How much has she asked for?"

"She wants a thousand pounds."

Kanwal took out his personal cheque book, and wrote a cheque for one thousand pounds. When he handed it to Sonia, she looked at in surprise. "Why do you want to give it to her from your personal account?"

"Is she not like my own daughter? Please Sonia, let me do it for her."

Sonia wanted to insist, but Kanwal put his finger on her lips. "Please, I don't want to hear anything more." His nearness brought a wave of disturbing exhilaration. So she hurriedly thanked him and left.

The day Neena and Narinder left for Kanpore, Kanwal brought his mother home, and Sonia became her constant companion.

Before the week was out, Kanwal got a trunk call from New York. Dr.Vincent Smith told him to bring his mother to New York, within a fortnight, as there would be a bed available for her.

Since Kanwal didn't want to leave Sonia behind in India, one evening after supper he asked her, "How about a stroll on the beach?"

"I'd love to go," she said unhesitatingly. She had missed his company all these days.

Kanwal held her arm when they crossed the narrow pathway to reach the beach. Accustomed to the terrain, he strode easily ahead, pausing now and then to let Sonia catch up. When Kanwal saw Sonia out of breath, he remarked, "Please sit down, I don't want you to get breathless." He then put both his hands on her shoulders and spoke seriously, "Listen Sonia, Dr.Vincent Smith has confirmed a bed for mother at the New York cancer hospital. I earnestly want you to come with us. I really need you."

Sonia looked at him. For days now she had acknowledged her love for him. She cared so deeply, she wanted never to leave him, even though it made her absolutely wretched to think about his promise to marry Ratna. Without betraying her feelings, she smiled at him and said, " I would be glad to accompany you. After all what are friends for!"

Kanwal couldn't help embracing her when he said, "Thank you Sonia."

For one delicious moment, Sonia relaxed in the pure joy of feeling his arms enfolding her. Then all her misgivings came crowding in and she quickly struggled free. Seeing pure terror in her eyes Kanwal's expression hardened. Sonia saw that his fists were clenched and she guessed she had dealt his pride a shattering blow.

# CHAPTER VII

A day before their departure for Rome, Neena was about to enter the drawing room when she heard her name. She stopped beside the door which had not been properly shut and heard her mother-in-law saying, "That uncle of Neena is a very clever person." There was a pause before Narinder spoke, "don't worry, Mom, as soon as I reach Rome, I'll get all the details of her inheritance and it would then be easy to have full control of it. It's just a matter of few more months."

Instead of going into the room, Neena tipped back to her bedroom. A few days after her wedding, she had a feeling that Narinder was after her inheritance, and over hearing their talk, her doubts were confirmed. She didn't know how she would be able to handle the situation. She had very little time to sort out her affairs, as they were flying to Rome next morning. She phoned her mother's aunt, and decided to go and see her.

Neena went to Prem's house and told her what she had heard, and asked her, "Do you think it would be a good idea to let Dr. Khanna know about it?"

Prem too agreed and so Neena rang up Bombay. Dr.Khanna picked up the receiver and getting the whole story said, "Listen Neena, we are leaving for New York early morning. Your mother has agreed to accompany us. At London we have a couple of hours stop over. I'll phone your attorney and ask him to draw your Will in anticipation of your inheritance. I think I'll be able to arrange it the way it will not only safe guard your inheritance but also your life. Don't give your husband any indication that you are aware of his intentions. The amount of wealth you'll be inheriting can turn any body's head."

"Please, uncle don't tell Mom. she'll start worrying."

"I won't, be rest assured. Good bye dear, have a nice time. After you reach Rome, phone Dr.Henry Northbrook and get my telephone number from him."

While Kanwal, Radha and Sonia were still on the plane, Radha had a mild heart attack. Kanwal personally looked after her. As soon as they landed at New York, Kanwal and Sonia took Radha to the hospital, where she was admitted into the intensive care unit. Kanwal also met Dr.Vincent Smith and handed him all his mother's test reports as well as the prescriptions for the treatment she had been getting at Bombay.

Leaving his mother in the hospital, Kanwal and Sonia left for the Palace Hotel, where they had booked two rooms. Sonia was greatly impressed by the luxury, grace and style of the fifty-one storey high rise hotel.

Kanwal then phoned Dr. Henry and told him of his arrival and his mother's heart attack on the plane.

"Would you like me to pick you up from the hotel?" asked Henry.

"There's no need for you to bother. I' have a friend with me. We'll both come and see you this evening if you have no previous engagement."

"Then do have dinner with us. My wife and I'll be waiting for you and your friend."

By twelve-thirty Sonia had showered and changed when Kanwal knocked at her door. "Come in, the door is un-locked."

Kanwal looked very attractive in cream pants and blue silk shirt open at the front. He asked,   "Would you like to go out to lunch or do you want to eat here?"

"I'm not hungry. I had a sumptuous breakfast on the plane. How about you?"

"In that case let us ask room service to send us something light. How about fried eggs, toast and coffee?"

After they finished eating, Kanwal left Sonia to relax. He also told her they were invited by his friend Dr.Henry for dinner.

At four thirty  Sonia came out of her room. She was dressed in a dark blue skirt and a matching blouse, and wore high heeled sandals. She looked very attractive in western clothes, light make up, and Her hair tied back loosely with a ribbon, that they fell in a shiny cascade to her hips. Kanwal couldn't resist staring at her for a few seconds.

She too couldn't help noticing how startlingly attractive he looked in the evening clothes.

They took the elevator to the hotel lobby and went out. Sonia walked fast to keep up with the stride of those long legs, her high heels clicking. Kanwal turned around, his face full of humour and charm. On reaching the pavement, Kanwal held Sonia's arm to help her across the road to the taxi. When they were seated in it, he noticed the door on Sonia's side was not properly shut. As he leaned across to slam it, she felt the weight of his legs against her, so she looked up at his profile. He looked so attractive that for once Sonia wanted to tell him how much she loved him; but her heart was full of bitterness at the realization that he didn't love her. She felt she could really hate him, and also despise herself for giving her heart to him. She consoled herself in her mind saying, "Let him waste his charm on that other woman," As these silent words were spoken her forehead creased with bitterness.

Once the taxi moved on a clear stretch of road, Kanwal turned and their eyes met. Sonia saw his expression change. The calm expression in his golden brown eyes were replaced by a look of shrewd probing enquiry.

Sonia forced a ghost of a smile, and to turn his attention away from herself she said, "I think I was once introduced to Dr.Henry."

Dr. Henry welcomed them. Henry looked at Sonia and commented " Mrs.Seth? It's years since I've seen you. But you haven't changed a bit." Before he introduced his wife Helen.

"Thank you. I'm glad to hear it."

After they sat down, Sonia looked around. The white stone exterior of the house and the narrow windows, had given no indication of the beauty within. Sonia was impressed by the glittering chandeliers sparkling down on floors covered with glowing soft rugs as well as the silk and velvet drapes that muted the hum of traffic.

"You have a beautiful place," she commented.

"Thank you, Mrs Seth for your appreciation." Then Dr.Henry asked Kanwal, "How is your mother?"

"Before we left, I phoned the doctor. She's better. Her blood pressure has returned to normal."

"How long are you going to be in New York?"

"Depends on mother's health." Then added, "The hotel I'm now staying is too far away. I wish I could get a nice place near the hospital."

"I have one place in mind. When you told me you were coming to New York for your mother's treatment, I had a talk with a friend who keeps house guests. He agreed to let you a room. I'm not sure if he has an extra room for Mrs.Seth. I'll have to find out."

After supper they all sat in the living room with cups of coffee. Dr.Henry looked at his wrist watch and said, "I guess, Father David must be home by now. I'll phone him and find out if he can accommodate both of you."

In about fifteen minutes Dr.Henry returned. "You are lucky. Father David has agreed to let both of you be his house guests. The house is in Greenwhich Village, just a couple of blocks from the hospital."

"I'm glad it's so close," said Kanwal, but I still need to rent a car."

"Those rental cars are not very reliable. My limousine is sitting idle in the garage. What about using it while you're here?"

"I'll be grateful for your generosity. Are you quite sure you want to lend me?"

"I really mean it."

"How can I thank you?"

"Please don't mention it. What are friends for?"

"I'll be visiting mother at ten in the morning. When should I go and meet Father David?"

"I'll phone him in the morning and let you know."

A taxi took Kanwal and Sonia back to the hotel, and Kanwal followed Sonia to her room. Since Neena's wedding Kanwal had been trying to be very impersonal, but tonight Sonia felt him to be quite different. At the door Kanwal said, "It's too early for me to retire, I'm going for a walk. Would you care to join me?"

"You are right. It is too early to go to bed. I think I'll come. She thanked her stars that Kanwal asked her, for she really loved his company.  At the elevator, Kanwal looked at her and remarked, "It's going to be cool outside. You should have brought your wrap."

"Oh, no, I'm quite warm. I love being able to go without a jacket."

"You need one," he insisted "The breeze comes so suddenly one never knows.....it can be quite cool on occasions. I'll fetch the jacket for you."

Was Kanwal really concerned for her welfare? or did he just not like her arguing?  Whatever the reason, Sonia wondered and before she could say, "don't bother, I'll go and fetch it," he was gone.

He put the wrap around her shoulders, before they left the hotel. They walked quietly for a while, inhaling the cool breeze, until Sonia stopped looking at some fine material in the showcase of a big department store. "She muttered to herself, "The silk looks pretty." and then started walking again.

They walked for another mile before they came to a bridge over the Hudson. Sonia eagerly looked at the enchanting scene, of a myriad twinkling lights reflected in the calm waters of the river. "Does it cast a spell over you too?" asked Kanwal with a smile. "Yes, it's fascinating."

Both of them stood there in silence, intent on the exquisite scenery, and there mutual love for beauty swept away all restraints and brought them close. Inadvertently Kanwal put his arm around Sonia's shoulders. A strange happiness for a second enveloped her, and she turned towards him. Kanwal too smiled in quick response as he gently drew her closer. The next moment she got startled and quietly moved away, and wordlessly they both walked on together. Sonia felt an inexplicable tightness in her throat, for she couldn't keep back her thoughts about Ratna, who had in a way, challenged her at Simla. Some times she got confused, for Kanwal never spoke about her, and he never talked about his pending engagement to Ratna as her mother put it. Some times she felt that Kanwal wasn't in love with Ratna but it could be a marriage of convenience, because she was the daughter of a chief minister. She suddenly came out of her reminiscence when a group of teenagers ran past them. She saw two police cars following, sirens screaming. Later the fugitives were surrounded, hand cuffed and taken away.

"They might have escaped arrest, if they had sneaked into those numerous lanes instead of running on the lighted road." Sonia remarked.

"I guess, they had no choice." Kanwal answered.

"I think they were stupid." Sonia remarked.

"You know, one has to have some place to escape to, but quite often there isn't any where to go, in which case the sensible course is to resign to your fate and accept what life has to offer."

"I don't think so." She murmured.

Kanwal heard her remark and couldn't keep quiet. He therefore commented, "Let me put it this way. Those young people accepted prison, actually they accepted a shelter which they otherwise didn't have. In other words they took what was available. But I can tell you there are people in this world, Sonia, who persist in trying to escape from life."

Kanwal's words hit her hard, because in her own case they were true. She had been feeling dejected because of her unforgettable past and sometimes she felt she had nothing to live for. In her case the future stretched ahead as an endless void, and perhaps Kanwal had sensed it.

His remarks confused her more. She thought perhaps Kanwal was trying to tell her, "You are trying to escape from reality, for you could ofcourse get a physical union from me, but nothing more. " These thoughts made Sonia feel upset and her brow creased in doubt. At the same time she couldn't resist arguing, and felt Kanwal was waiting for a comment from her. So she said with lot of force, "I still don't follow what you are trying to tell or justify."

"Don't you?" His tone was clipped and impatient. "Very well, let's forget it."

They walked back to the hotel in silence. As they entered, the setting sun bathed the granite pillars of the lobby in a deep crimson glow that contrasted eerily with the dark background. As they stood waiting for the elevator, Kanwal looked at her, "Tired" he asked with a mingling of gentleness and concern in his tone.

Out side her room Sonia said brightly, "Thank you for the wonderful walk," but her eyes told a different story. Tears threatened to choke her, and the kindness in his eyes when he left her with a goodnight, did nothing to help her.

Later as she lay in bed, she wondered exactly how Kanwal felt towards her. He certainly desired her but did it go beyond that! She also remembered the companionable ease with which they had walked, and stood on the bridge admiring the scene that had brought them closer. Finally she closed her eyes, inviting sleep to come.

When she opened them again it was day light. A frail sunlight was fingering its way hesitantly across the walls. There was a sound of knocking at her door. She hastily got up, slipped into her robe and went to open the door.

A waiter stood there with a tray of hot steaming coffee, bread rolls and cookies. She just told the waiter to put it on the side table. Before the waiter left, Kanwal walked in. She saw he was casually dressed in cream pants and a blue silk shirt half open in front. He thanked the waiter for bringing in the early coffee, and closed the door before he turned to

Sonia, "Good morning, I, hope you had a nice sleep." Then looking at the tray, he said, "They smell good."

"Would you like to have some?" "Thank you."

Sonia went back and propped herself with pillows before she poured the coffee. Kanwal followed her and instead of taking a chair, perched himself on the side of the bed and held the cup. Sonia glared at him, then immediately felt foolish, when a wide grin spread across his face. "Before I went for an early walk, I ordered the early breakfast. I see you perhaps didn't want it. You are an enigma, Sonia with all your changing moods. One second you are smiling, the next you're frowning. Did I offend you right now, to have you look at me so annoyed?"

Sonia lowered her eyes, unable to hold his gaze. "I know I am a bundle of nerves these days. I'm sorry. It was really thoughtful of you to have ordered this early." Then holding her cup and taking a sip she asked very casually, " What are we going to do today?"

By ten o'clock I have to be at the hospital to see mother and meet Dr. Smith.  Will you be all right on your own?" He asked anxiously,

"Can I come to the hospital with you instead of just sitting here." "Sure."

Then Kanwal stood up, "thanks for the hot coffee and rolls. I'd better go and get ready. We'll leave by nine forty five."

Sonia too went to shower and dress. Since she had reached New York she had mostly worn trousers. That day she chose a plain blue silk saree with a matching blouse and petticoat. The day had been getting warmer, but rain was forecast for the evening and consequently the temperature would cool down.

As soon as they got into the taxi, he put his arm around her shoulders. Sonia found an unexpectedly warm look in his eyes, and felt a tenderness in the way his fingers moved across her shoulders, gently kneading her flesh. His face was so close she could see the pupils of his eyes, golden brown with tawny lights. It was just like studying someone on the television screen, with the camera lens; and trying to enter the heart of the man through his features. Yet his face didn't give anything away. Her love for him made her ache to respond. How she longed to strike the dark crisp hair, to touch the strong neck that rose from the square shoulders. But she reprimanded herself to keep her senses in control. She had realized she was a fool to have given her heart to a man who would never want to marry a woman with such a heart aching past, even if he forgot about Ratna. But she was quite sure that even if she ran away from him, no matter where she was, her thoughts would always be with him; because he was mentally reaching out and drawing her to him like a pin to a magnet. Kanwal looking into her eyes Said,"My mother and I seem to have invaded your life, the last couple of months. I hope we haven't caused too much disruption?" Then he pulled her gently into his arms. It was so unexpected that her defenses were down and she remained quiescent. He did not go further, just went on caressing her gently, encouraging her by his very control to abandon her remaining fear of him.

"My mother loves you, so she confides in you readily."

"You know your mother better than I do," Sonia said casually. "We all see each other with different eyes," He said quickly.

His arms that were still around her were surprisingly light and unusually gentle. Although the morning was a bit chilly, Kanwal was not wearing a coat. Sonia could hear the hammering of his heart and felt enveloped in his warmth and strength. She longed to believe there was something deeper than mere desire between them, which wasn't true. He was a man of the world, used to women's attention and it would not require any effort on his part to be completely relaxed with her as with any other woman. Once she would give in, there could be a whole life of misery ahead. At this sobering thought she slowly moved away from him. It was not so strange to find out that she could so easily arouse him, for earlier she had taken him to be a man of iron control. But iron too has its breaking point. She admonished herself for thinking of him, or reading too much into a few gestures of affection, and behaving like an immature person. She bitterly acknowledged that the word love was wrong. If she thought that was what had prompted him to keep her with him, she was wrong. He just needed her for a little while, so long as his mother needed her company. She frowned at the thought.

Soon they were at the hospital. Radha was in bed. She looked better. Seeing them a little smile lit up her pale face and she spoke very softly, "I'm better," Sonia held her hand and sat down on the chair beside her bed.

Kanwal left them and went to see the doctor. The two men discussed Radha's case. Eventually Dr. Smith said, "I'm afraid the leukocytes have again increased enormously. I'll have to start chemotherapy immediately. I'll also have to increase her blood hemoglobin to counteract anaemia. Tonight we are giving her a complete blood transfusion."

"Can we come to see her in the evening?"

"It would be better if she is not disturbed for a couple of days. You can always look at her through the glass door."

"O.K. Doctor, thank you." Kanwal heaved a deep sigh.

"Dr.Khanna, don't worry, I promise to   try   every thing

possible to save her."

Kanwal returned to his mother's room. He heard Sonia say his name but as soon as he came in, she stopped talking.

"It's all right, Mamma, you'll soon be well. Dr.Smith wants you to relax for a few days. You'll not be allowed visitors. Please don't worry. I'll be in the hospital every day to find out about your treatment."

Radha put her hand on his and caressed it lovingly. Kanwal too kissed his mother's hand and said, "Mother, will it be all right if I go out to see a friend? I'll be back in an hour. Meanwhile, Sonia will give you company."

Radha nodded. He then made a gesture at Sonia before he left.

Dr.Henry met him at the hospital lobby. They both left in Henry's car. "Father David would be expecting you in the evening.. He has promised to keep your rooms ready. I'll get you the car right now, so that you are mobile."

"Thanks Henry, for all your wonderful help."

Kanwal returned to the hospital within an hour. His mother was resting and Sonia sat by the bed reading a magazine. Before they left, he assured his mother, he would come to the hospital regularly to find out about her treatment and welfare, until she is allowed visitors.

Radha gave a fleeting smile and closed her eyes with a slight nod. Kanwal and Sonia went out to the car. Having helped Sonia into it, Kanwal started the car and then looking sideways, he said, "By now, Neena and Narinder, must have reached London."

"I hope they are enjoying themselves, sight seeing."

"As soon as they reach Rome, Neena has promised to phone." Then looking at his wrist watch, he remarked, "Since we go to see Father David in the evening. We have almost the whole day to us. How about going to see the Statue of Liberty, the most important land mark of the states. On the way, Kanwal said, "I appreciate your help and sacrifice in leaving all your interests back home. I really mean it."

Sonia kept quiet. She was looking at the scenery, with gardens filled with exotic plants that cast seductive perfumes on the breeze. She couldn't resist saying instead, "Look at those gardens with flowers every where."

"A little stroll would be quite exhilarating." Saying this he parked the car and both of them walked towards the big garden. They roamed about silently and sat down for a few minutes to inhale the fresh scented air. Later they walked into Montague Street, a narrow thoroughfare lined with restaurants and shops. Unhurried, and in the same atmosphere of harmony and companionship as on their walk last evening, they strolled towards the cafes with their alluring smell of food.

"Shall we sit here? Taking her acceptance for granted, Kanwal pulled out a chair. Sonia had the breathless sensation of living in an unreal world, somewhere on another planet, as she had for that moment, completely forgotten her past or future. When they finally left the cafe, Kanwal drove her arm through his and although he did not say any thing, Sonia derived a strange comfort from this simple gesture. He once again helped her into the car and they drove off in silence.

After a few minutes, Kanwal abruptly stopped the car near a big department store and got out, saying, "I'll just be gone for a few minutes." When he returned, he had a big bundle in his hand. Sonia looked at him in surprise, "You seem to have done a lot of shopping in these few minutes."

His answer was short. "I needed a few things."

They were now heading for Battery Park. As soon as they reached there, they could see the Statue of Liberty standing majestically on Bedloe's island, at a distance, sending a message to Americans and the whole human race to know and enjoy the precious fruit of freedom. They got out near the ferry terminal to take the round trip on the Staten Island ferry.

Kanwal and Sonia went on gazing at the Statue of Liberty. Kanwal's hands dropped to her shoulders in a friendly, automatic gesture, but Sonia quivered under his touch. She hoped he hadn't noticed. It's beautiful...I'm so grateful to you, for bringing me here," she confessed. "I did want to see it."

"Then why on earth you didn't say so?" He looked at her.

"Your mother is so sick, I didn't want to distract you. I know how you feel, and actually we aren't on a sight seeing trip after all."

"I think I know what you are trying to say." and a slight pressure on her shoulders was a subtle way of expressing his satisfaction at her reply.

Sonia knew that was no time for intimacies, but as curtsey demanding, she said, "Thank you Kanwal."

Back in the car Kanwal looked at the city map to find Greenwhich Village, because New York is the most complex city in the world; its size and diversity challenge even the most intelligent and well travelled person.

They reached their destination and rang the bell. Father David opened the door and smiled, "I guess you are Dr.Khanna and Mrs.Seth. Do come in. I hope you found my place easily."

"O, yes. The way Dr.Henry gave the direction, it was easy to locate it."

Father David took them to the living room. Sonia liked the set up. He showed them their rooms which they found quite cosy and neat. There was one bathroom that opened on both the sides, which Kanwal and Sonia were to share. A big balcony, brightened by plants and flowers, some hanging and some in tubs on the floor, stretched outside both the rooms. Each room had a single bed with nice soft sheets and comforters. The windows were large and attractively curtained. There were nice soft rugs. And each bedroom had side tables and a small couch, a dresser with an oval mirror, and the closets were commodious. As they entered the kitchen, Sonia saw it had a stove, refrigerator and a dishwasher. The cupboards were stacked with dishes, pots, pans and cutlery. Father David also told them, "I'm busy most of the day. My work takes me out any time. I would like you to feel at home and cook whatever you feel like eating. I have a part time help for the house hold chores. She comes every evening to wash and dust the suite. Every other weekend she cleans all the windows and trims the garden. She'll be in, any moment. I'll introduce her to you."

While they were still talking the bell rang and Father David went to open the door. He came back accompanied by a woman in her late fifties. Father David said, "Wendy, meet Dr.Khanna and Mrs.Seth. They are my new house guests."

After they exchanged greetings, Kanwal brought his and Sonia's bags from the car and put them in their respective rooms. Sonia went to her room and then on to the balcony. Under the balcony she saw a small garden bright with flowers; and beside it a few shady trees. She stood there, her thoughts straying towards Kanwal. She felt that being in his constant company had inadvertently, awakened in her a curiosity to learn more about his attitude towards life. At the same time she was in fact quite depressed because she couldn't open up herself and make him aware of how she felt about him. She had no choice but to hold back her feelings for him, realizing that he would certainly reject her, not only because of Ratna, but he already knows about his husbands impotency and would want to know who fathered her daughter Neena; for which she herself had no idea and was constantly in pain, and it would not be possible for her to tell the true story, which she didn't even tell her husband, instead left him the moment she knew he was impotent. Seeing all her dreams being shattered due to her innocent past, tears rolled down her cheeks...and found them being wiped away by a snow white handkerchief. Then putting his arm around her, Kanwal said tenderly, "Sonia, what is wrong? Can you not confide in me? You know I'm your friend, and always will be."

She looked up and forced a ghost of a smile and then gently pushed him away. Kanwal was only being polite and sympathetic. This time her reaction annoyed him. "Why do you want to turn and run whenever I come near to console you? Do you think I was making a pass at you?"

Flushing, Sonia muttered something inaudible, annoyed with herself. She knew her love for him had made nonsense of logic. There was no doubt about his anger, as his face was tight and his golden brown eyes had a brightness that was due to rage and not excitement.

Instead of apologizing to soothe him down, she said, "I think I'll go back to my room." just making him aware of her own ego. As she turned to go, he regarded her with an intense and curious expression and held her by the hand. She glanced at him in surprise at his sudden change of mood. Instead of anger, his face wore a smile of amusement and he laughed lightly. "Are you sure you want to be alone for the rest of day?" His gaze slid to her lips, as if his intentions were obvious.

Sonia knew her weakness and so wanted to leave but felt too choked to utter another word. Kanwal went on slowly, "You've been different since you came back from the hospital."

"Please, Kanwal, I'm tired. Let me go in and rest."

"You are an odd person, Sonia. I wish you'd stop bottling things up." Then with the cold politeness with which she had become familiar whenever he tried to keep her at a distance he said, "Very well, I shall never ask you to confide in me."

Sonia turned away. How could she confide in Kanwal, how could she tell him what was wrong? She hastily went in leaving Kanwal confused and baffled. "You're a wary little fish, aren't you? He murmured to himself."

Once back in her room a feeling of emptiness drained away all Sonia's strength. She lay down and her dark head moved restlessly on the pillow. She felt her life was just a kind of story one reads in an old magazine.

Kanwal stood where she had left him reminiscing. He enjoyed Sonia's company; and for the last couple of months they had been constant companion. He knew she had both a lively mind and a strong sense of humour, not to mention a good deal of intelligence. In her company even his mother's illness didn't worry him much. He was sure a life without her would not be worth living. But since he had seen her bridal dress, he had his doubts of which he never wanted to think about. Even then he tried to be very careful. He was quite sure, he must at all cost keep his feeling under control if he didn't want to lose her for good.

When he went back to the living room, Father David was

ready to go out. He said, "I've some urgent work. I won't be in till midnight. I hope you'll help yourself to supper."

"Don't worry, we'll manage. See you in the morning."

"Breakfast will be at eight thirty. If you are used to morning tea or coffee, help yourself."

After Father David left, Kanwal prepared tea, and with the tray knocked at Sonia's door. She opened the door and stood looking at him for a few seconds before she said, "Come in. Why did you bother? I was getting ready to make some tea for both of us."

"Does it matter?" He said and then handing her a cup,"I'm sorry, Sonia for my high handedness."

"Sonia held his arm, "Please forgive me. I too am very sorry. I don't know what happened to me."

Kanwal held her hand in his and kissed it and said with a laugh,"I've sealed it with a kiss. The war is over." Then putting his cup back on the table, "Wait a minute, I'll be right back."

He returned almost immediately with a package and handed it to Sonia with a bow. "What is it?" She asked, astonished.

"Open it and see."

Curiously, Sonia opened her parcel to find a beautiful saree. It was the one she was admiring the night before in the window of a department store. She looked up both pleased and touched. Kanwal with the cup was about to go to his room when Sonia said, "Kanwal please don't go. Sit down and finish your tea." When she said this her face broke into a beautiful smile. "How did you know I liked this silk?"

"I saw you gazing at it last evening. It's not a big deal, just a small token of good wishes from me and my mother."

"Thank you, Kanwal."

Later sonia cooked supper for both of them. At ten she said

goodnight and went to her room, undressed, washed and got ready for bed. The silk saree was still lying there. She picked it up, holding it against her cheek to feel its softness, and lay down to sleep. The sound of the wind moving the branches of the trees out side was very soothing. She felt light hearted for once.

## CHAPTER VIII

Next morning Kanwal woke up early and decided on an early morning run. Returning back he made tea and carried it to Sonia's door.

"Good morning, Kanwal, do come in." Sonia took the tray from him and motioned him to a chair. "How confident and self possessed, he looks." She wondered if there'd ever been occasion in his life when he lacked that cool composure. As he stretched his hand to hold the cup she was handing him, she was again struck by the beauty of his hands...large, but so finely shaped, with their long fingers and spatulate nails. then her eyes moved up to the light blue shirt that clung damply to his ribs, and the half exposed chest with its mat of crisp dark hair.

While sipping tea Kanwal remarked, "I was out jogging just now. It was quite pleasant, but I did get rather warm." He mused as he had been aware of her eyes on him.

In confusion Sonia looked away and concentrated on drinking her tea. Kanwal put down his cup and before he left for his room he said, "Father David wants us to have breakfast at eight thirty. I'll be going to the hospital immediately after. Would you like to come with me or do you want to stay back and have a quiet day?"

"I'll come with you."

"See you later." He then picked up the tray and left.

At the breakfast table Father David wished both of them good morning and enquired about Kanwal's mother.

"She's still not out of the woods. You know how painful is the chemotherapy, which she is under going."

"Pray for her. There is more power in prayers than in anything else."

"You are right," said Sonia."

At nine thirty Kanwal and Sonia left for the hospital. They watched Radha through the glass door. She was lying still. They stood there about fifteen minutes and then went to see the doctor.

"Dr.Khanna, I assure you, she'll be better in a fortnight."

"When can I go and visit her?"

"She'll be allowed visitors by tomorrow afternoon."

Back at the car, Sonia could see how Kanwal felt depressed in spite of Dr. Smith's assurances. She couldn't help saying, "I know how you feel about your mother, but you too are a doctor and you know it takes time to pick up strength. Why don't we go and pray in a church. Don't you remember what Father David said?" Then impulsively she put her arm around his shoulders.

"If...if you wish." Kanwal's voice sounded flat and dejected. He took out the route map and started looking for a nice church. Sonia knew him well enough to realize that in normal circumstances his pride wouldn't let him show any weakness.

Kanwal drove to Trinity church just off wall street. There was an organ recital going on. Kanwal and Sonia both sat quietly, with their eyes closed, to let the majestic soothing music flow over them, while they were in prayer. This helped a lot and when they left they felt quite strong.

"How about visiting some other churches?" Kanwal suggested.

Sonia nodded in agreement. "We can go to St. Paul's chapel and St Patrick's Cathedral."

Kanwal especially liked St.Paul's church. He told Sonia that George Washington used to come to worship there. At St.Patrick's cathedral they both knelt down and as in other churches prayed for Radha's recovery.

It was noon and Kanwal said, "How about going for lunch at Delmonico's?"

"Is that a special restaurant?" asked Sonia.

"It is the meeting place of the elite of lower Manhattan. The building itself is also worth seeing."

After lunch when they emerged, Kanwal said, "I want to go back to the hospital at five. We have a few hours. Why not go and relax by the river. For a while thay stood on brooklyn Bridge. It gave them a splendid view of the city; and the bridge itself was a remarkable engineering feat.

"How high is the bridge from the river?" asked Sonia.

"The guide book says, one hundred and thirty three feet. It's also over a mile and a quarter in length."

Kanwal also showed Sonia the Empire State Building. Some day, after mother gets well, I'll take you up to the one hundred and second floor, to see the building bathed in coloured lights. This is the only way for the city to commemorate holidays and special occasions."

Then they went down to the river and strolled for some time along the bank. Neither spoke, yet the silence between them was not in the least constrained. But when Kanwal suddenly held Sonia's hand to steer her around a wet patch of sand, he felt her quiver. "You are quite safe, I assure you."

Sonia looked up at him. With the sun glinting in his eyes

and his dark hair, she couldn't read his expression, but she was quite sure, her behaviour had hurt his feelings. She felt bad for annoying him for it was too late to realize that he really wanted to help her over the heavy, muddy ground. At the same time she was intensely conscious of his nearness and of his hand still holding hers. She wanted to free her fingers but he didn't loosen his grasp. Helplessly she looked at his face and saw that although he was smiling his eyes told a different story. She was quite sure that Kanwal was just being considerate; nevertheless his nearness affected her profoundly. It sparked an exquisite throbbing fear that left her heart in a tumult as she was no more sure of her strength and could give way, to her feelings, which at all cost she wanted to avoid, so as soon as the muddy patch was over, she disentangled her hand from his and abruptly edged away; although she sensed the change come over him due to her sudden behaviour.

Kanwal got confused at this reaction. He was no more sure what Sonia really wanted. At times she was so transparent, but most of the times he knew she was trying to hide her feelings and she did succeed in it. He really didn't know what she wanted. Did she want that kind of a platonic relationship or did she want more? He wondered about it for the rest of the day; as these thoughts never left him even when he was in the hospital.

That night in bed Sonia talked to her self, "How cruel fate is? If I had only learnt about Kanwal's impending relationship to Ratna a little earlier, it might have kept me from admitting my love for him. How can an emotion once discovered be forgotten to leave me heart free." Sonia wondered where Ratna was these days. She knew very little about her or her work. She could only guess that she was definitely older than Neena. Did she really love Kanwal or was she ready to marry him for his wealth and position. All these thoughts had started crowding on her.

Thinking about her feelings for Kanwal, she was genuinely scared of betraying them for whenever they were close her knees turned to water and her confidently voiced independence evaporated. Even then she promised to herself to keep her feelings hidden from him at all cost. Eventually she drifted off to sleep.

By the end of a fortnight, Kanwal's mother felt better as her condition had improved, and when Sonia and Kanwal went to visit her she was sitting up in bed, looking well groomed with her hair combed back smoothly, although her skin still was pale.

Kanwal smiled at his mother and asked, "How do you feel?"

"How do I look? I'm feeling much better."

"What does the doctor say?" asked Sonia.

"The doctor want me to sit up in bed, any time I feel like sitting up but he doesn't want me to strain myself. He has promised to let me have a wheel chair within a week."

As soon as Kanwal left the room to consult the doctor, Radha anxiously looked at Sonia and said, "Did you speak to Kanwal about his engagement to Ratna? And what did he say?"

"Mrs. Khanna, all that I gathered from his talk, he's worried about your health and is waiting for your recovery. Please, don't think about it just now. I'm quite sure as soon as you are well, he'll do what you want and definitely get engaged to Ratna, no sooner you are back in India." Sonia said a little hesitantly, as she didn't have the courage to ask Kanwal about it, and so had to lie to her.

"Are you quite sure?"

"No, but I just have a hunch."

Twenty minutes later, Kanwal returned, smiling, "The doctor says if your progress continues, you'll be discharged in almost two weeks. But we'll stay in New york for the next couple of months, so that he can watch your progress."

Radha smiled weakly before she spoke, "You look as if you're about to catch cold. Go home and rest. If you're not feeling good don't come to the hospital tomorrow. I'll phone and let you know how I'm feeling."

As Kanwal was slightly feverish when they reached home, he spent the rest of the day in bed. Sonia served him lunch and supper in bed.

Next morning when she brought the morning tea to his room, she found him still fast asleep, with his right foot peeking out of the blanket. To her astonishment she saw a birth mark, a small blue star right below Kanwal's big toe, like the one her son Neil has at the exact spot. She went on looking at him. In sleep he looked younger. A stubble of unshaven beard darkened the chiselled angles of his face. The hair that was normally combed back from his tanned face now fell across his forehead. She felt his forehead, The fever was gone. At her touch he opened his eyes and looked into her smiling face.

"Good morning," he said huskily.

"Good morning, How about a cup of tea?"

He sat up and took the cup from her. "Thank you. What would we Khanna's do without you? You are an angel of mercy to us."

Sonia blushed in appreciation.

As Kanwal rubbed the stubble on his chin, Sonia wondered if it would be very rough to touch. She felt a longing to put her fingers against his face.

Kanwal smiled at her, "Miles away, aren't you?"

She looked up at his remark and met his amused eyes. Then she hesitantly said, Kanwal, may I ask you something?"

"Of course, go ahead." he said leaning back against his pillows.

"Today, when I came into your room, your right foot was showing. I noticed a mark of a blue star under your big toe. Is it a birth mark?"

"May be, but why are you interested in it?"

"Does any one in your family too has it?"

"To be more precise, it's said to be a heredity mark. Although it's funny, but all the male members of my family, my grandfather, my father, had it and so my younger brother also has it.

My father told me that even my great grand father had it."

Isn't it funny, Neil has the very same mark exactly under his right toe."

Kanwal sat up with a jerk. "What did you say?"

"My son Neil has the same blue star, under his right toe." Sonia repeated.

Kanwal put his hand over his eyes. Finally he said very slowly. "Did the hospital tell you who was Neil's biological father when you were artificially inseminated."

"I was never told of being artificially inseminated. I only found out when Varinder threatened me of taking away my son as he professed to be his biological father, that I confronted my husband, and you know the rest. "Yes, you told me about it."

"Do you know when were you artificially inseminated?"

"I don't know the exact date, but I remember it was just after the day when I first met you at the club."

"Are you quite sure?"

"I'm positive. That is why you never saw me again in the club, till we again met at the hospital Jubilee party."

* * *

Kanwal vividly remembered the day he had first met Sonia in London. It was the last day of his internship, and he had gone to the club to get a book he needed for his job interview next day, to get a job in the same hospital where he finished doing his internship. He was confused but then he thought may be this could be just a coincidence or who ever was Neil's biological father might have the same mark and they might be related to our family, many generations back.

"What are you thinking, Kanwal?"

"If Varinder, as he says is Neil's biological father, he might be related to my family, not now but some generation's past. Such a situation might be rare, but it's possible."

"In that case Varinder should also have such a birth mark?" Sonia exclaimed.

The news did upset Kanwal, but before he could decide to find out more about it, the phone rang. He picked up the receiver. His mother was on the other end. "How are you today? Kanwal?"

"I'm feeling better. How are you?"

"I'm fine. I phoned you to say, you don't bother to come, if you still have cold, because the doctor doesn't want you to visit me for I can be an easy target."

At the breakfast table Sonia said, "Father David, a few days back I read in a tourist guide, that New York's ethnic ghettos are often stringently maintained by the residents, who live within their boundaries. I'm curious to see them. Can you suggest how I can go their?"

"Please Sonia, don't try to go there by yourself, for it's dan gerous. Whenever my work takes me there, you can accompany me."

It was a warm Sunny day. After Father David left, Kanwal lay down, with a book, under the sun in the garden at the back of the house. He read for a while and then dozed off to sleep. He was feeling much better when he woke up and went in for lunch. After lunch Sonia too came out and went to sit under an olive tree which was in a corner of the garden near the bed of yellow daffodil's and deep red tulips. She went and sat on the circular stone as she didn't want to be anywhere close to Kanwal for sometimes his mere sight made her extremely self-conscious. Even sitting at that distance, she was thinking about him, and how much she wanted Kanwal to love her. Her heart was always where he was. It was tempting her to go to him and say anything, just to hear his voice....and yet her pride and her circumstances wouldn't let her do it. She could see him from that distance absorbed in reading his book. She was unaware of the fact that the book he held was a mere pretence. Instead he was watching her every movement. His heart went out to her, but he too had his own pride.

While still reminiscing another thought popped out in Sonia's mind; since they both lived under the same roof and were constantly in each other's company, proximity might gradually make him come to care for her. Of course that meant she would have to give some sign of her feelings for him. By now Sonia was quite sure that he wasn't really in love with Ratna. He was going to marry her just to please his mother, and the chief Minister, Ratna's father. She finally decided to make an effort to find out about his feelings for Ratna, as soon as an opportunity arose.

Before she went in, she looked back at Kanwal and for a

moment their eyes met, but she soon turned away and closed the door behind her.

## CHAPTER IX

For the last couple of days, Kanwal had realized he could no longer pretend to be casual with Sonia. He therefore was trying to be near her as much as possible without making her feel nervous or out of line. In fact he very much wanted to see a smile on her face. Since Sonia's remark about his birth mark he had decided to go to London. When Kanwal came indoor, he saw Sonia sitting on the couch looking lost in deep thoughts. Lately he had found out that no matter where she was, she was always brooding, and it could be on her past, as she had herself confessed several times.

Kanwal came and sat down beside her. She looked at him, "How are you feeling now?"

"I'm fine. Actually I'm tired of sitting home for the last forty eight hours. Would you like to go out with me tonight. We can just go around and watch the city tonight, with all the lights."

"I'd love to go. Are you sure you are okay?"

"O, yes, I am."

"Then, let me go and make some tea before we leave."

Sonia brought the tea tray in the living room. After they finished drinking, leaving the tray on the kitchen sink for Wendy, she went in to get dressed. It was strange for her to feel she should look her best when going out with him. So after her shower she slid into a soft turquoise-blue dress with a layered skirt, short sleeves, and a low cut round neck. She was also careful with her make up, as well as her hair do.

She let her hair fall in a ripple like a heavy fall of satin, and still its rich lustre could not be denied.

When she came out Kanwal was waiting, in a cream coloured suit with a self designed shirt and a black tie. Sonia thought in that out fit he looked even taller, and his tanned face even more angular. As always the sudden confrontation with so much overpowering masculinity left her groping for something to say.

Kanwal had no such problem. He fixed a glance at Sonia. "You look beautiful in that dress," he said, "You might attract lot of attention tonight."

Though she knew he was teasing her, she couldn't help the swift colour that flamed in her face. She turned abruptly to go down the steps to avoid her blush, but Kanwal stepped along with her. Suddenly she stumbled, and he at once put out a hand to steady her. Excitement had given colour to her cheeks, and they heightened the creamy pallor of her skin, making her eyes glow like forest pools, dark and fathomless. "Watch yourself," he chuckled. She was intensely conscious of his nearness as usual, for he was still holding her hand. Once outside, he helped her get into the car before he sat behind the wheel, and drove off.

First Kanwal stopped at an East Indian shop at the department store where he bought several sarees. Then he went in for a very expensive lady's and a gent wrist watch. He asked Sonia to select some dresses for he knew she had a good taste, when it comes to clothes. Before she selected them she had to ask, "For whom are you buying these? Please don't misunderstand me, I can only select them properly if I know."

"They are for friends." He said putting his hand on her shoulders to show his feelings for her better taste.

After the shopping, Kanwal drove to India House on the south side of Hanover Square, and the old custom buildings which were built in neo-classic style.

Soon it started getting dark. Near the Brooklyn Promenade, he stopped the car and they both got out to admire the sun drifting down to the western horizon and the lights of Manhattan shimmering across the east river. Kanwal took Sonia's hand, "from here," he said, "You can get an idea of the magnitude and beauty of this city. Look at those towers of The World Centre rising over lower Manhattan, and the Brooklyn Bridge spanning the river on your right. When you look north, there is the Empire State Building and the United Nations Secretariat, both mid-town landmarks."

Back to the car, their next stop was at Shizan, the most beautiful Indian restaurant in New York. It was a beautiful place. The tables were laid with spotless white linen and the silver ware gleamed attractively. After consulting Sonia, Kanwal ordered the special tandoori mix, an amalgam of small helpings of almost everything on the menu. Instead of beer, he ordered fruit juice. The dessert consisted of Rus Malai,*  They ended the meal with a cup of hot tea. with cream and sugar.

"That was lovely," Sonia looked at him across the table and smiled. "Thank you, for bringing me here tonight."

As they were leaving, they were offered betel leaf with many ingredients in it.

Back in the car Kanwal drove to Battery Park, with its twenty one acre of green over looking New York harbour. Both of them walked down to the statue of Giovanni de Verrazano, the pilot of the Dauphine. From there Sonia could see the ship's light flicker golden points far off on the

* A preparation of cottage cheese and cream

horizon under the star filled sky. The moon hadn't yet risen, and it was quite dark outside, but not dark enough to hide the white tips of the waves as they curled and broke to the shore.

Sonia's head slowly dropped to rest against Kanwal's shoulders. For once she didn't retreat, thinking One day who knows she might be free of pain. It seemed natural for Kanwal's arm to encircle her. They both watched the moon appear in the purple dome, to be swallowed up by a patch of cloud, only to reappear as the cloud broke up apart and reveal the pearl tinted heavens.

Sonia felt the time was right to question Kanwal further for Radha's and her own sake. "Kanwal, do you mind if I ask you something?"

"Don't hesitate."

"Don't you want your mother to feel happy?"

"Sonia, there is nothing I want more than to give my mother whatever she wants or needs. You know I love her very much."

"Then why don't you make her happy?"

"I don't understand you."

"Of course you do; but you're so secretive." She said this but wasn't sure if she had offended him.

"Now you're being unreasonable," he said a little hesitatingly. "How can I know every thing my mother desires?"

It was now Sonia's turn to pause. She didn't know just how to tell him. "Why can't you tell your mother you'll get engaged to Ratna and get married to her as soon as you reach India." She blurted out.

Sonia felt his hand tightened on her shoulders; then slip down her arms unsteadily. She felt being pulled closer and his arms tightened around her. Inadvertently when she lifted her face to his, he released her so suddenly that she staggered.

In the moonlight she could see how his fists were clenched. "I'm sorry Kanwal, if I went too far?"

Please Sonia, I don't think it's a suitable time to discuss my life, right now. You know I promised mother I'll get married as soon as she recovers. I know my mother is getting impatient." He then turned around to put his arm cross her shoulders. "Sonia, lets drop this subject for good, till then."

The absence of emotions with which he had spoken convinced Sonia that he would tell her nothing. She became quiet as they drove home. To humour her Kanwal said, "What deep thoughts are going on behind those wide brows of yours?"

Sonia too flashed him a brilliant smile, and Kanwal became aware of the gamin quality about her. He didn't for a moment suspect that the smile was forced, and that he had a bigger advantage over her than any man ever had- even not her late husband.

When they reached home, he simply followed her to her bedroom door and said goodnight.

At the sadness in his voice Sonia longed to tell him she would try to give him her companionship he wanted, but the shyness kept her silent. She merely gave him her hand, said goodnight, and closed the door.

Next morning, when they went to the hospital they found Radha sitting on bed. She had a smile on her face as she looked at them. Kanwal noticed that there was even more colour in her cheeks.

"How are you feeling today?" mother, when he sat down beside her on the bed and holding her hand, Kanwal asked very softly.

"Much better. I feel new strength seeping into me." Then very casually she added, "I asked the doctor when I can go home? He told me that if my recovery continues, I most probably would leave the hospital within a fortnight."

"That's a good sign. You better take lot of care and rest as much as possible." After a few small talks Kanwal said, "Mother, something important has come up, and I therefore need to go to London for a week. I'm leaving tonight. Is it okay for you, if I leave? I'll phone you every day from there. Sonia is here and she'll visit you every day."

It was news to Sonia. She looked surprisingly at Kanwal and asked him, "When did you decide to go away? You never told me about it."

"I know, I should have told you, but I first wanted to find out about mother's health, before I could be sure about it. Till then it was just a tentative program. Last evening after you retired, I got a phone call from my lawyer and I told him I'll let him know if I am able to leave mother and come. It all depended on how she feels. Now that she is better, I've just decided to go."

"I hope it's nothing serious."

"It's just about my properties in England, and I've got a good deal to dispose off some of them. I might even be back earlier, if there are no complications."

After the visiting hours, Kanwal and Sonia left. While driving Kanwal felt Sonia was lost in her thoughts. To humour her, instead of going home he drove to Brooklyn heights, a place of gardens and got down. "It's early. How about a walk in the garden for some fresh air."

Sonia nodded and stepped out. Kanwal put his arm around her and took her to a bench among the flowers. She was afraid to look at him, lest tears might spill down her cheeks.

Since he knew her to be upset, he pulled her closer. "I understand you are upset, for my not telling you about it. I'm sorry. The work is really very urgent and I'll be back soon." With these words he wiped away her tears with his handkerchief.

Sonia looked up, "You knew all the time that you were going to London. After all you bought all those things. Don't tell me you only decided last night after I retired to bed."

"Of course I was in touch with my lawyer and I knew the deal would mature any time so I was just getting ready. The only thing that was stopping me was mother's health. Now that I feel she is on the road to recovery, it is quite safe to leave her and go." Then he gave her a fleeting kiss before he said, "Listen Sonia, I never want to hurt your feelings. I'll try my best to serve you, the way you would want me to, to the best of my ability."

It was late afternoon when they reached home. Father David was in. He enquired about his mother from Kanwal. Later Kanwal told him about his plan. He also gave Father David his address and telephone number, where he could contact him in case of emergency. While they were still talking the telephone rang. Father David picked up the receiver. "Just a moment," he said and handed the receiver to Kanwal. "It's for you. You can pick up the extension in your bedroom. It's from Neena."

"How are you Neena? I'm pleased to hear from you."

"I'm fine, uncle. We've reached Rome. How is Mom?"

"She's fine. Would you like to talk to her?"

"Yes, but first I want to tell you something. Mr.Lawrence Smith, the lawyer from Smith & Smith, has come to Rome to buy a house for us. I've seen the place. Dr.Alphonzo helped him get a nice place. We'll be moving there in a week.

The interior decorator and an architect have already finished the work, I wanted it to be done.

Mr.Smith has also shown me several cars and I have picked out a small vaxhall for myself. It will be at the door tomorrow morning. I've also taken a Roman driver's license. Thank you uncle, for making all this possible."

"You are welcome, darling. If anything else you need, just ask Dr.Alphonzo, and he'll provide. By the way, I'm leaving for London tonight. Should I send the Watsons to Rome?"

"Yes, please. They can stay in the guest house. It's been furnished."

"Did you get my letter?"

"Yes. It served the purpose well enough. When Narinder read the Will, at first he was in rage and he questioned me, as to why you got such a Will drawn? But when I told him that you and Mom wanted to safeguard my interest, as they didn't know anything about him, he calmed down. He now knows,in case of my sudden death within the next ten years, the property will revert to my family....my mother and later to my brother. Since then he has changed quite a lot. He's become more considerate and caring. I guess he realizes I'm the goose with the golden egg."

"Look Neena, I know he is money minded, but if he's properly treated, he would be a nice companion."

"Uncle, I've started a part time job in the hospital; because I used to get bored sitting athome. There's one more thing I need to tell you."

"What is it?"

"When we were in Paris, Narinder ran into his elder brother. His name is Varinder. He used to be a pharmacist in a London hospital. Do you know him?"

"We thought Narinder was the only son."

"Varinder is his step brother. He left home when he was eighteen."

"I see. How does he appeal to you?"

"I didn't like him. You know he has invited us to London for the next long weekend."

"Neena, I know him. He is not a good person. Try to avoid him. Please don't accept his invitation. Also don't let him know you are Dr.Rajinder's daughter. He didn't have good relations with your father. Be very careful of him."

"But how can I avoid him?"

"I'll phone Dr.Alphonzo to make sure you are on duty the day Narinder plans to visit him. Take care of yourself. Hire a chauffeur, some one reliable, who can also act as your body guard. Listen, rich girls have to be very careful these days."

"Thank you, uncle. Can I talk to Mom?"

Sonia talked to Neena for sometimes. Kanwal was pacing the floor. Sonia guessed he was upset. "Is something wrong?"

"Neena met Varinder at Paris. He is Narinder's older brother."

"But Prem told me Narinder was the only son."

"Varinder is his step brother."

"Are you sure he is the same person?"

"Yes, I know he worked as a pharmacist in the same hospital where Rajinder and I worked. Neena has confirmed it."

"He is very clever and cunning. I'm afraid he'll do anything to blackmail her."

"I'm quite confident, once I tell Dr.Alphonzo, he'll definitely protect Neena from him. He's already got Neena a house in his neighbourhood where he can keep an eye on her. Don't worry, Tonight I'll request him to engage a reliable body guard-cum-driver for Neena."

Kanwal's London flight was at eight thirty. Dr.Henry promised to give Kanwal ride to the airport. Sonia insisted to see him off. Kanwal put his arm around Sonia's shoulders and softly pulled her close. She looked into his eyes, when he said, "I hope you'll take care of my mother. Dr.Henry has promised to drive you back and forth from the hospital. Neena has promised to phone you daily, and if by chance you don't hear from her by evening, you should phone and find out about how things are going on there."

Sonia just nodded. The mere thought of not seeing Kanwal even for a few days loomed ahead of her like a black void. She suddenly realized That a whole life without him would be unbearable. She felt helpless trapped by her own ungovernable emotions in a situation that could yield her nothing but further pain.

That evening Sonia retired early; to the privacy of her own room, and picked up a book. Outside the wind had increased in fury and a few drops of rain had been followed by a violent hail storm. She read and re-read a page of the book, but still didn't know what it was all about. She put the book away,and with her hands behind her head, once more began to think about Kanwal. She was certain Kanwal found her attractive and desirable. Lately he had been opening up; but he never by words or action tried to show her that he loved her. Her reverie was broken by the angry shrieks of the wind, and the lash of the ice pellets against her window. She remembered that Father David had told her at supper that the storm warning had been issued. She prayed for Kanwal's safe journey, and turned off the lights before she fell into deep sleep.

A week later as usual Sonia got a telephone call from

Neena. "Mom, when is uncle due back in New York?"

"He's coming by the evening flight today. I got a call from him from London, early morning."

"Mom, when have you decided to come to Rome?"

"Kanwal's mother will most probably be discharged from the hospital in a fortnight, but we still have to be in New York for a couple of months. When she and Kanwal leave for India, I'll come and stay with you for a month before I go back to India."

"How is Niel? Have you heard from him?"

"I talk to him every weekend. He's fine and doing well in his studies."

"Say hello to uncle. I'll call you tomorrow again at this time."

"Has Gladys come to Rome with George?"

'Yes, They came a couple of days back. I like the couple. They both are very considerate and certainly look after our needs. Goodbye Mom, talk to you tomorrow."

"Goodbye, sweetheart. Give my love to Narinder."

At four thirty Dr. Henry was to pick up Sonia for the airport. She sat in the living room waiting his arrival. She looked excited when Father David entered the room. "When is Dr.Khanna arriving?" he asked.

"By the six o'clock flight."

"Dr. Khanna is a good person. I'm glad you both are good friends. You know, I too have missed him."

"Since my husband died, he has been looking after my family; just to honour Rajinder's last wishes."

"He's not only intelligent, rich, attractive, but also a very good person. I wonder why he's still a bachelor?" Father David asked a little curiously.

"I don't know. According to his mother, he left home very

early, went to England, studied medicine and settled down there and never once returned home till a few months back. But now he has promised his mother to marry the girl of her choice as soon as she is well, and they return to India."

"And suppose he loves some one else, will he still marry the other woman?"

Sonia looked at Father David with surprise before she questioned him, "Why do you say so?" Before Father David could answer, he got a call and so he left abruptly with an excuse.

When Kanwal got down from the plane, he saw Sonia and Dr.Henry waiting for him. He came forward, shook hands with Henry, "How are you, old chap? why did you bother? I would have taken a taxi?"

"What are friends for?"

"Thank you."

"Please don't mention it. Did you have a nice trip?"

"Yes, it was quite interesting." Then he hugged Sonia and asked, How are you?"

"I'm fine."

"How is mother?"

"She's improving."

Back at the priest's house, Father David welcomed Kanwal. Later when Dr.Henry left and Father David retired for the night, Sonia too stood up to leave. Kanwal's hand reached for hers and held it lightly. "Please, sit down. Isn't it too early to retire?" And before Sonia said something or sat down, Kanwal took out a letter from his pocket and handed it to her. "Niel gave me this letter, to hand it to you the moment I reached New York."

With a look of surprise she said, "Where did you see Niel?"

"In Simla, at his school; where else?"

"Are you telling me, you went to India?"

"Yes, I had to go there, for a reason.?"

"To meet some one?"

"Yes, some one special."

Kanwal's words stabbed Sonia's heart. She was sure, he had gone to meet Ratna; otherwise why would he ever go to Simla? But to hide her feelings, she asked casually, "How is every one in India?"

"Karan and Anju are working hard. I got them engaged at a brief ceremony. She is a very attractive, intelligent and a good influence on Karan. They are both in the final year of M.B.B.S." Then added slowly, "I was surprised to see how much Niel had grown in just a few months. He's now only a couple of inches shorter than I. I also met his teacher. They are happy with his progress at school. He is captain of the junior hockey team." Then he pulled out two photographs he had taken of Niel. Sonia was delighted with them.   "Did you visit my place? How is Gopal?"

"Gopal is fine. He sends you his regards."

"How long was your stay in Delhi?"

"Just twenty four hours, only for Karan's engagement as he and Anju both insisted. When mother gets the news, she'll be very happy."

By ten thirty Sonia got up. Kanwal too rose with her. "I'll walk you to your door."

Sonia said goodnight to Kanwal rather stiffly. It was difficult to sustain an appearance of indifference when her emotions were involved.

Once she lay down on her bed, she couldn't sleep. She was thinking of that other woman. The thought of her as Kanwal's wife engulfed her in a terrible feeling of despair. She got out of bed and, striving to calm herself, tiptoed out onto the balcony. She didn't notice Kanwal there until he caught her hand in his. Startled she whirled to go back, but found her being pulled close to him.

Slowly his hand traced the outline of her face, his thumbs lightly brushing her lips, before his hand settled on the curves of the neck. Sonia's resistance was melting as swiftly as the wax of a lighted candle. Her iridescent eyes glistened with the tears she was trying to hold back. She wanted to whisper, "I love you! I love you!" but how could one cross bridges when they hadn't been reached?

Even in that turmoil she couldn't keep her eyes straying to the gaping front of his robe, and that mat of hair which she knew reached down to his naval. Before anything happened, Kanwal had a second thought and to avert the situation he said with a grin, "How about raiding Father David's kitchen?" I could do with a cup of coffee and may be you could too."

Sonia nodded wordlessly. After the coffee, he led her back to her bedroom, with his arm around her and her head resting against his shoulders. At that moment Sonia felt like a child being comforted and protected. He tucked her in bed, kissed her forehead lightly, and left at once, closing the door softly behind him.

Next morning when they were at the breakfast table, Father David asked Sonia, "Do you still wish to see the ghettoes?"

"Of course, I do."

"At about one o'clock, I have some work at a church in the centre of that area. How about accompanying me then?"

Sonia looked at Kanwal, who nodded. "We'll be back from the hospital by noon, so we can easily join you."

"I'll be in by twelve thirty. See you then."

At the hospital Radha was happy to see Kanwal. He just

told his mother about Karan's engagement to Anju; but didn't say a word about visiting Simla.

"I'm glad about Karan.

"Mother, your would be daughter in law is a fine young woman."

"I know. but what about you?"

"Mother, I'll talk to you later about me. Right now I'm only thinking about what is good for you. Please don't misunderstand me. Take it easy. There's plenty of time to discus my life." While he said this he looked at Sonia.

Radha didn't insist for she thought he didn't want to discus about Ratna in Sonia's presence. She therefore smiled and said, "Of course there is plenty of time, as soon as I am home."


## CHAPTER X


As scheduled, Father David drove Sonia and Kanwal towards Bedford Sturvesant in Brooklyn. On the way, the priest told them,"On this road there are more murders than other places in the world." Sonia and Kanwal looked at him in surprise, to hear him talk of murder and death so coolly.

Further down, they noticed trash that littered both sides of the road, and the smell of dirt. They also saw groups of teen agers in dirty and tattered clothes moving lethargically hand-in-hand. Most of them were black.

"I...I...never dreamt of seeing such a sight in America." said Sonia falteringly. After a pause she said, "We do have this kind of poverty and dirt around the slums in India."

"There are poor and homeless people in America too. But the condition of these youngsters is not due to poverty. It's drug addiction that has reduced them to this. Some of them ran away from home and others were thrown out."

As they drove on, Sonia saw a group of youngsters dodge behind a wall. Soon they heard sirens and two police cars appeared. The youngsters ran away and hid in a back yard. The police went after them and while the others ran away, they came out with two, a boy and a girl. One policeman was carrying a plastic bag. They virtually had to drag both the kids to their car and thrust them in.

"Why are the police after them?" questioned Sonia.

"Those particular youngsters are agents of drug smugglers. They get all sorts of drugs, such as marijuana, hashish, L.S.D., cocaine,opium, and heroin from them and sell them to other youngsters, not just in ghettoes but also in schools and universities. In fact they are the ones who help to spread addiction as well as disease like aids."

"That's dreadful. Can't it be stopped somehow?"

"The authorities try a lot; but you know the problem is world wide. In the States many philanthropic societies, government agencies, religious groups and some individuals, all try to lessen its impact on the nation,by helping with men, and money to fight the addiction. The interpol is another group that works at trying to catch the smugglers."

As the car drove into Clinton Avenue, Father David stopped the car in front of a house. He got out and asked them, "I have an important job to do here. Would both of you like to help me?"   "of course, we would love to."

As they got down, they saw beside a heap of garbage, five boys from a street gang standing there leaning against a fence. One of them pointed at Father David and shouted, "Hey, Jerry, that's the preacher who's been trying to help me."

"Get lost, preacher,"said Kenny haughtily. "You and your books. We don't want to hear it, do we Jerry? Man, doesn't he know we're junkies?"

"Shut up, Kenny,"said Jerry. "it's O.K. He ain't gonna make us read that Bible, even though he is a halleluja man."

Father David went over to them. "Look, sons, you are all loved by the Lord. Why can't you understand? Trust me. What I say is true."

"Okay, what do you want?"

"I don't want anything. I'm here to protect you. Look at that guy. He's trying something that could kill him. I just want to help save him."

"Do you all want to come in?"

"Yes. And these two friends from India, would also like to come in."

Jerry who seemed to be the leader, took all the three of them into the building. The hall way was dark and smelled strong of urine. Father David along with Sonia and Kanwal climbed four floors to the roof and stood at a place a little distance away from the four teen agers, three black boys and a white girl with blonde hair. One of them had a coke bottle full of murky looking water. He took out a mettle bottle cap, a lighter, a piece of rubber tubing and a syringe. He dipped the needle in the bottle, and before he could take it out, Kanwal reached there and caught his hand. "What are you doing?"

"Leave me alone! I'm sterilizing the needle."

"In that filthy water?" asked Kanwal.

"Any objection? If you are chicken you'd better just beat it."

Father David, who stood watching, nudged Kanwal, and shook his head, indicating not to interfere. The boy then took a bag of white powder from under his hat and poured some into the metal cap. He then held the lighter under it, until it melted, before he drew it into the needle of the syringe. Finally he wrapped the tubing around his arm till the vein swelled, and injected the liquid.

The next boy did the same. Sonia looked away saying very softly, "I can't stand any more."

Father David took her aside, "very soon they are going to lie down. Then we have work to do. We'll take them down to the shelter, in the basement of this building. Once there, they can be helped to get out of this agony."

It took the entire gang at least thirty minutes to inject themselves with the drug.

Father David thanked Jerry for showing them around. We'll leave now. We've seen enough."

"So you too are chicken, preacher. Well, we too are leaving pretty soon, as we also have an important work to do."

"What do you do?" asked Kanwal.

"Preacher knows what we do. We have to get more customers."

"Why do you do that? You know you're only shortening your lives, and those of others."

"Who cares! We gotta have bread to survive, and if we ever try to get out of it, we'll meet with an accident and die before our time."

Kanwal, Sonia and Father David stayed on the roof out of those children's sight waiting for the drug to take effect. It wasn't long before all the four kids were in a stupor.

Father David was expecting help. Soon two black men came to join them. The four men picked up the kids, none of whom looked more than thirteen years old, and carried them down to the basement. Sonia followed them. Unlike the rest of the building, the basement was neat and clean. Father David rang the bell and a man in his forties opened the door.

They went in and laid the children on clean tidy beds.

Sonia looked around. The basement had been converted into a church. On one side stood the altar with the cross. Candles were burning on it. On the other side, behind a screen were ten beds. three of beds were already ;occupied, and the new patients took up another four.

All the men busied themselves stripping the dirty clothes from the bodies of the kids they had just brought in. Sonia attended to the girl, sponging her with clean towels and lukewarm water, putting a clean dress on her, and brushing out her tangled hair.

Father David said, "Thank you Sonia for your help."

"Please don't mention it. I am glad I was present here. I am shocked to see their plight. What do you think would happen as soon as they come out of the stupor? Won't they just run off again?"

"Hughes has already telephoned the police. They'll most probably take these kids to juvenile prisons, and keep them there till there parents or guardians come. And if they don't turn up or disown them, these kids will be kept in these centers until they are cured of their addiction. Here they'll be getting good food, medical aid, and the service of a psychiatrist, and will be taught some useful trade according to their capabilities. Our job is to get hold of as many of these young addicts as we can and see that they are in right hands. This building will gradually be converted into a reform house, because it's an ideal spot, right in the centre of the ghetto."

"As long as I'm here in New York, may I help you?" asked Sonia. "I too would like to help these children." Said Kanwal.

"Splendid. So far very few doctors are available. You would be saving many lives."

Next day at breakfast Sonia asked," Father David, I've been thinking how so many kids are getting addicted.?"

"I've been working with them for the last five years. Every day there is a different story."

"I'm just curious. Can you tell me some that you know."

"Some of them get hooked as young as eleven. I remember a story of a black boy whose name was Thomas. I rescued him when he was fifteen. At first he wouldn't tell us how he got into drugs. After staying three years in Auburn State Correctional Institute, he came out completely cured. It was only then that he told his story. He was just eleven when one of his friend, the same age, named John, one day brought a cigarette and offered him half of it. Thomas having never smoked, just wanted to try for fun sake. From that day onward, John would bring a cigarette and both of them would share it. After a month, when Thomas got used to smoking, John stopped bringing it. When Thomas asked why he wasn't bringing any more cigarette, he told him that he had used up all his father's cigarette, which he had stolen and he couldn't get hold of any more; but he could take him to the person who sold that kind of cigarettes.

Since Thomas wanted to smoke, he brought some money from home and aggreed to buy the cigarette. Soon he was smoking one cigarette a day. By the time he was thirteen, he started spending all his pocket money on it, and when that wasn't enough, he had no choice but to steal things from home and sell them to buy the cigarettes. The person who sold him told Thomas he could get ample supply of cigarettes if he brought new customers. Thomas allured some of his friends who also in turn got addicted and made others pay for their addiction. Soon his behaviour changed and his grades started going down. Some how his mother who was divorced found out, and she was bent upon reforming him, and so she contacted me. Some how we got hold of the boy and put him into reform house. That's just one story, and one of the many methods used by the drug agents to entice  the children and sell their wares. It's a vicious circle that goes on and on."

"Can I go to see these juvenile prisons?" Sonia asked earnestly.  "I would really like to help the young girls there if I'm allowed. Please let me know whenever you need my assistance."

"Thank you Sonia, for volunteering. As a matter of fact, I'm going to this reform house right now. Would you like to accompany me?"

Dr.Kanwal and Sonia both agreed to go and accompanied Father David. When they reached there, they found out that the police had recently brought three young guys, two boys and a girl, all between the ages of fourteen and fifteen. Father David followed by Kanwal and Sonia went in. He showed them the whole place, explaining how it functioned.

When it came time to leave for the hospital, Sonia was still busy. "Would you like to stay and finish the work?"

"I want to. Can't you wait a little longer as I also want to go and see Radha."

"You can go to see her in the morning. Mother would understand. You take your time. I'll pick you up at seven thirty in the evening."

Kanwal found his mother in bed. "Are you okay, Mother?"

"I feel tired again. I also have a slight pain in my abdomen."

"Did you tell the nurse to inform your doctor?"

"Yes, I did. He came to examine me. He thinks, I must have strained myself sitting up long." Then looking around asked, "Where's Sonia?"

Kanwal explained what they had been doing and why Sonia had to stay back. Finding Kanwal alone, she said, "Did you phone Karan about your safe arrival?"

"Yes, I did." Then added, "Mother, are you happy to hear about Karan's engagement? Your would be daughter in law is a fine young woman."

"Of course, I am. What about you? Did you go to see Ratna? You never told me anything about her."

"Ratna wasn't in Simla. She got a job in Madras. I didn't have time to go there."

"Did you see Ratna's father?"

"No, I couldn't."

"Look Kanwal, you know quite well I've promised Rai Hukum Singh to make Ratna my daughter in law. Before I die, I want to see you married."

"I don't love Ratna. How do you expect me to marry her without love, at my age?"

"In arranged marriages love comes later."

"I'm close to forty and have stayed abroad for so long, I can't even think of getting married without loving the person. Moreover Ratna is half my age. How can you expect me to marry her?"

"Don't you know she loves you. What does it matter if she's too young. You know she too is a doctor."

Kanwal was silent. He didn't have the courage to contradict his mother. He saw her pale face go paler. He also couldn't tell his mother he loved Sonia and life without her was not worthliving.

Seeing her son not saying anything but sitting quietly, Radha took his hand in hers and softly said, "I know what your problem is?"

"What do you know?"

"You were quite willing to marry Ratna before you met Sonia."

"Please, mother, you are not well let's not talk about it, right now. Actually I don't want you to bother about me. Just relax and try to recover."

"I guess you're in love with Sonia. Am I right?"

Kanwal looked at his mother and nodded. "I knew it. But can she remarry? Will her mother and her daughter agree?"

"I know it's not easy."

"Since she too loves you, why do you think it's difficult?"

"You might be right. But I'm still not sure about it?"

"Just ask her to marry you, and you'll find out."

"How can I ask her? you just told me yourself, there could be problems due to our culture."

"I think it would be quite easy if you both decide to live abroad."

"Please mother, let me manage my own life."

Hearing these words Radha took away her hand from his, abruptly as a gesture of anger.

"Mother, I know you don't like to hear this. Remember, I love you very much. So long as you are sick I can't think straight. Once you are well, we'll talk about it. For now just forget about my problems." Then looking at his wrist watch he stood up. "Sonia must be waiting for me. I have to pick her up. I'll come tomorrow and talk to the doctor."

Driving back to the reform house, Kanwal was upset, and scared that his mother might tell Sonia about his feelings for her. He knew that he won't be able to face her, once she finds out the truth and is unable to reciprocrate due to her long unforgettable past which is still bothering her. However hard he has tried, so far she hasn't been able to confide in him, about who was Neena's biological father as he knew her husband was impotent.

He then mumbled a few words to himself saying,....."if what I think is.....true...then what! What a tangle." Kanwal was scared. He was so absorbed in his thoughts that he lost his way. He stopped his car on a lonely roadside and waited. Soon another car came along and stopped to see what was wrong. Kanwal explained, and got directions to get to the reform house. He arrived quite late, to find Sonia anxiously waiting. As soon as she saw him, she exclaimed! " Thank God you are safe. I was worried to death."

I'm sorry. I would have been in time, but I lost my way. I owe you an apology for keeping you waiting."

"I don't expect you to apologise. You are not familiar with these roads. It could happen to any one in your situation."

"If I had been paying attention, this wouldn't happen."

As they drove home, Sonia put her hand on Kanwal's shoulder and said, "I guess you are upset. Is your mother all right?"

He looked at her before he spoke, "She isn't so well. She has again complained of pain in the abdoman."

"What do think, it could be?"

"I'm afraid for her. The symptoms are not good. I'm really scared."

"Please Kanwal, don't get disheartened. She is in good hands. Just pray for her."

When they reached home, Father David had already retired, but their supper was left warm in the oven.

"I want to wash and change." Sonia said, "I've been helping kids who really smelt pretty bad."

After supper they took their coffee into the living room and sat down watching T.V.

Feeling Kanwal's eye on her, Sonia looked up. To avoid his

stare, she asked, "Did your mother enquire about me?"

"Yes. I told her what you were doing at the reform house. she appreciated it."

After supper they were still sitting in the living room when the phone rang. Kanwal picked up the receiver and asked. It was from Dr.Smith. He told Kanwal that he had increased his mother's dosage of medicine as her leukocytes had abnormally increased. The dosage didn't suit her and her blood pressure was not stabilizing. He should be at the hospital as soon as possible.

Kanwal put down the receiver and told Sonia about it.

By the time they reached Radha's room, her condition had deteriorated. The doctor had lost all hopes. She was actually on her last breath, and her eyes were closed. "Mother, please, look at me." Kanwal pleaded.

She opened her eyes. He put his hand in hers, while Sonia's hand was on her chest. Radha tried to  move Kanwal's hand closer to Sonia's. He understood what she was trying to do. When she put Kanwal's hand into Sonia's, she drew a deep breath, and was gone.

There were tears in their eyes as Dr. Smith drew the sheet over her face. "I'm sorry." He told Kanwal. I tried my best; but I couldn't save her."

The body was taken to a room close to the hospital chapel. Kanwal brought wreaths from the hospital shop and he and Sonia both placed them on her body. They also lighted candles. Kanwal then phoned Father David, gave him the news and asked him to come and pray for his mother's soul. Sonia sat down beside the body and read the Bhagwat Gita of Lord Krishna, which she brought it with her.

Within an hour Father David arrived to pray for the departed soul.

Next day the body was cremated and the ashes were put in an urn. Kanwal phoned Karan and gave him the news, and told him that he was sending her remains by a special messenger service to Delhi. He should take the delivery and go to Haridwar to submerge them in the  holy Ganges. He also told him he would be back in India within a month.

Every thing happened so suddenly; Kanwal felt his world was crumbling around him. He was so dazed, he would sit for hours saying nothing. Dr.Henry and his wife tried to take their minds off that grief by inviting them to be their guests for a few days.

On the second day of their visit, when they were in the kitchen talking to Eva, Sonia suddenly became dizzy, and felt as if blackness was enveloping her entire body. She reached out, grasping at the air. Seeing this, in a single leap Kanwal sprang to catch her, and gathering her close against his strong body, he carried her off to her room.


## CHAPTER XI


With the help of her two friends, Darshan and her husband sukhwinder, Neena was able to move into her new home. She also joined her part time job at the hospital, in spite of Narinder's objection, and as he couldn't stop her, his male chauvinism had had a set back.

On the first day, at the hospital, after Neena had completed her round and was leaving the ward, she met Dr.Alphonzo and Dr.Mohan. The latter looked at her and stopped abruptly. "Hi, Neena, what a surprise to see you here?"

"What are you doing here?" she too asked in surprise.

Dr.Alphonzo, looked from one to another and said, "Do you know each other?"

"We were class mates back home." Mohan said.

"That's very interesting," and before he could say more Neena excused herself saying, "see you later." and left abruptly .

When she came out of the hospital, Paul was waiting for her beside the car. Paul Longfellow was black. Dr.Alphonozo had known him and his parents since Paul was a toddler. He was not only reliable, he was also a good driver. He had asked Neena to hire him as her diver cum body guard.

On her way home Neena started thinking of Dr.Mohan and how tall, slim attractive and handsome he looked. She remembered how good humoured, sensible, lively and well behaved he was during their college days. Today the feel of her handshake gave her a queer feeling, when suddenly her body vibrated in quite a different way. Then other thoughts of her new life, her job and about her mother cropped up and she forgot all about it. She was a little worried about her mother as she had phoned her twice but no one picked up the phone. She knew something was amiss as her mother had never before gone any where without informing her. To ease her mind she decided to ring up Dr.Alphonzo first thing in the morning to find out about Dr.Khanna.

Day light was streaming through the chinks of the curtain when Rose Mary, her personal maid, brought a tray of tea. While sipping tea she rang Dr.Alphonzo and said to him on the phone, "Sorry doctor, for disturbing you. I've been phoning Dr.Khanna in New York, but there is no answer. Have you heard from him?"

"Yes, Neena. Dr.Khanna's mother passed away day before. He couldn't get you on the phone, so he asked me to let you know. Yesterday I tried to tell you at the hospital, but you seemed to be in a hurry and you left. I also phoned you in the evening but you were not home."

"I had gone out with Narinder, and came quite late. I'm sorry to hear about Dr.Khanna's mother. Are they still at Father David's place?"

"No, they are at a friend's place. They told me they'll be coming to Rome any day, as soon as they can.

"Thank you doctor, you've relieved my anxiety."

"Are you attending the eye camp today?"

"Yes. I'm supposed to help Dr.Mohan."

"Tonight is the grand party for the doctors who have come from other countries to attend the camp. You must come. Bring your husband too."

"He's gone on temporary duty, and won't be returning by the evening; but I'll be there."

"After the eye operation camp, Neena arranged with Dr.Mohan to pick her up at her place that evening for the party.

Dr.Alphonzo introduced Neena to many doctors of other countries. She liked to be at the party as she had missed such entertainments after she got married. She therefore made up her mind to enjoy while she could. She danced with some of the doctors who had come from abroad, until Dr.Mohan asked her for a dance. Neena had no reservation, for during college days she used to dance with him very often. While they were dancing, a hand tapped Dr.Mohan's shoulder. "May I have the privilege of dancing with this lady."

Neena looked up and was startled to see his step brother in law Varinder. Mohan let Neena go, and Varinder put his arms around her. "I can't believe it's you Neena," he exclaimed. "You look so very different in western dress."

With his hands on her shoulders, he tried to pull her closer. Their touch sent a shiver of dislike through her. But soon she moved from his closeness obtrusively, and for the sake of curtsey and to make conversation she asked, "When did you come to Rome?"

The faint wrinkle of distaste on her brow did not escape Varinder, but he merely smiled. "Come, little sister let's just have this dance and then I shall tell you everything."

Neena reluctantly danced with him, loathing his nearness. His hand on her back kept moving past her waist, and she had to suffer it. At last the music stopped, and she heaved a sigh of relief. She came and sat down amidst some of her colleagues where there was little chance of Varinder coming after her. Before she left, she thanked Dr.Mohan for the ride and told him, " Paul brought my brother-in-law and I'm going home early, for he has some important work to do, before he leaves early morning."

"You don't look happy. Are you O.K. If you need any kind of help, let me know."

"Thank you very much. Please don't worry. I've already told Dr.Alphonzo and he thinks, family comes first. Any way Paul is there and so I guess I have nothing to worry."

In the car Varinder said, "Are you quite sure Narinder is not coming home tonight?"   "That's what he said."

"I told you I have to go back by the early morning flight. Is there any way I can contact Narinder?"

"I have no idea where he is staying? Can you not leave the message? I'll tell him to phone you as early as possible."

On reaching home, Neena took him to the living room. She sat down just opposite him on a chesterfield facing her step brother-in-law and asked, "I assure you he'll get your message and do whatever possible."

"I have no other choice. The problem is; I have to go to court, both in England and in India, for the custody of my son. I want legal help from Narinder. I want to know on what grounds I have better chances of succeeding."

Neena looked at him in surprise. "I didn't know you ever married."

He laughed. "That's true. I'm a free bird enjoying full life."

Neena let that remark pass without any comment, but the shadow of worry momentarily darkened her brow. With a forced smile she asked, "Then how do you happen to have a son?"

"It's a long story. Thirteen years ago, when I was working at the St.Paul's hospital in London, the department of research in eugenics asked many of us to contribute our semen for the purpose of research. Later I came to know that my semen was used to artificially inseminate a woman whose husband was sterile. She got pregnant and gave birth to a boy. Since the death of his so called father and grand-father, this boy has or will be inheriting a big estate. If I claim my son, naturally I'll become his guardian and then I'll be able to protect his estate for him."

"Varinder looks shady enough for any chicanery." Thought Neena, before she said with her eye brows raised looking straight at him. "You just said that many of you contributed your semen. How can you be sure that yours was the one they used? How can you prove it? And to do that you'll need lot of evidence."

"Luckily, I got hold of Dr.Rajinder's diary, in which he wrote why his wife Sonia had to be artificially inseminated with another man's semen."

Hearing her father's name Neena was stunned. She grew pale. Only then she realized why Dr.Khanna told her not to let Varinder know her father's name. Realizing its importance, she soon took hold of herself and asked, "Does the diary give the name of the biological father?"

"No. That's the only snag. I know Narinder is quite clever and he can help. I'm quite sure Rajinder must have asked them to select one from his own culture, and there were just a couple of us who contributed."

"Do you know who the other person was?"

"I couldn't find out. Since Narinder did his law in London, he might get the information."

While they were still talking, Paul brought in two cups of coffee. He handed one to Varinder and one to Neena. Neena held hers with trembling hands and said, "What time do you want Paul to take you to the airport?"

"Does Paul stay close enough?"

"He's not only my driver, also my bodyguard. He stays in the room next to mine. At night no one can cross his room without activating the alarm system."

"I see. You live like a little princess. When Narinder told me you are an heiress, I didn't believe him. I can now understand how you live so well. He is a lucky guy to have you." Then Varinder stood up. "Where do I sleep?"

"Paul will escort you to your room. Just tell him when you want to leave."

"Goodnight little sister."

"Goodnight."

Neena ran upstairs to her room, took off her green brocade dress, slipped into her kaftan and flung herself on her bed, after having taken the precaution of locking her door.

Varinder's way of eyeing her and never missing an opportunity of a pseudo-brotherly touch whenever she was within reach, made her positively writhe with dislike. She found him to be the most objectionable, horrible, conceited and insolent man she had ever come across, for the way he behaved with his own brother's wife. She remembered, while dancing he hadn't missed a single aspect of her appearance, and she had an angry bitter suspicion of the way he had been picturing her, like being stripped by a man's eye. She heard girls talk about such a feeling, but she never ever dreamt of its happening to her especially with such a horrible libidinous old beast. He wasn't in the least kind, sensitive, or understanding, and would never allow sentiments to interfere with his motives. She felt uncle was right when he warned her that Varinder could be ruthless, especially where money was concerned.

Then she started thinking of what Varinder had told her about the artificial insemination. If what he says is true, how come mother never told me about it. Why did she keep this secret from me. What if I too was artificially inseminated. But that wasn't just possible for the time I was born, no one new about it. Neena remained restless for the whole night, thinking of several reasons that could have left her father sterile and so the need for artificial insemination. She at last decided to go to London to have a first hand knowledge of all that happened there.

Early in the morning Neena phoned Dr.Mohan. He answered sleepily, but when he found out who was on the line he sat up abruptly; and said very anxiously, "What is it Neena? Are you okay?"

"Yes, I'm fine.I'm sorry to disturb you at this time of the morning. I tried to contact Dr.Alphonzo, but he was not available, so I had no where to turn to, except you."

"Neena, you know I'm no stranger. What are friends for. Please let me know what's wrong. I know you sound upset."

"You are right. Something very important has come up. I have to go to London immediately. My day is off. I wish you could come with me."

"Luckily, I too have a day off today. Of course I can come with you. What is it?"

"I'm still not sure about anything and that is why I need to go there to find the truth."

Mohan sensed she didn't want to confide in him, so he didn't insist. He just asked her on the phone, "When do you want us to leave for London."

"Can you come to my place, as soon as you can? Or should I send Paul to fetch you?"

"I'll be there within fifteen minutes."

"Thank you. See you soon."

After she put down the receiver, she sighed and walked across the pretty chintz hanging in front of the long casement window. Sunlight streamed in outlining her slender blue-clad figure and glinting on her smooth silky coronet of light brown hair. She couldn't help worrying. Thoughts again started crowding. She talked to herself, "What if her father had been sterile from birth, how could he have been her natural parent? or did something happen to him after her birth?" She'll have to wait to ask her mother; but she can definitely find out about her brother. When Mohan reached, she just told him about the artificial insemination of her brother, and she wanted to find out who was his biological father, for she couldn't believe a word that Varinder had told her.

After they reached Heathrow airport they took a taxi to St. Paul's hospital. She met sister Mary. Neena introduced herself and said, "I am Dr. Rajinder's daughter. Did you know my father?"

"O, yes. How can I forget him. He was a good friend. I'm really sorry to know he died in air crash. Where is Sonia? She too became a good friend, when she was in the hospital. I liked her very much."

"Sister, I've come to find out, who is the biological father of my brother Niel, Sonia's son."

"Isn't it funny, you are the second person in a fortnight who has come to enquire about Niel's biological father? But I'm really sorry, I have no idea."

"The hospital should be maintaining some kind of record."

"That's true, but they are confidential. Only Sonia or Dr.Rajinder can have excess to them."

Neena then wrote a name on a paper and giving it to the nurse said, "If you can't tell me the name, can you just confirm if this person was the biological father. And if he isn't just return me the paper and say nothing."

"Okay, Neena, as your mother was a very good friend, I can at least do this for you."

A few minutes later, sister Mary came back and gave the paper back to Neena."Thank you sister, for making my day."

"I know how you feel. I'm glad that we couldn't use him for Sonia. I clearly remember, why we didn't use him."

"Can you just tell me why?"

"His RH. was negative and Sonia's was positive."

"Thank you, sister."

"Are you working in London?"

"I work in a hospital in Rome, and this is Dr,Mohan, my colleague. We'll be here for the night and fly back early morning."

After they came out of the hospital Neena felt very light hearted. As she walked along, beside Mohan, she was conscious of his tallness, his leanness, and the suggestion of controlled strength beneath the well cut jacket. She found herself chattering on nervously, and for once, not at all sure of herself than she ever remembered being in life.

## CHAPTER XII

When Kanwal lay Sonia on the bed, she was still unconscious. He took out a bottle of smelling salt from his first aid kit and tried to bring her around. After several minutes she opened her eyes.

"How long have I been out?" she asked feebly.

"Just a few minutes. What happened?"

"I don't know. There was blackness before my eyes. I must be tired, and that's all I can think of." She said putting her hand to her head. Her head felt heavy, and it was too much even to speak.

"I know it has been a trying week. First those drug addicts and then my mother's death. I'm not surprised that you finally broke down." Kanwal sounded anxious, and at the tenderness in his voice she looked up at him with a watery smile. Though she was aware of him wiping away her tears, she made no attempt to confide in him. She had no mind to tell him why his mother, before she passed away had put her hand in his; for she was quite sure he understood it but was trying to ignore it intentionally, and that hurt her feelings. But keeping all her thoughts and emotions to herself she said, "What good have I done by accompanying you to America? I guess, I've just been a responsibility and nothing else."

"Now stop thinking about yourself being a burden. You know you're intelligent and good. You've stood by me and helped me keep my wits intact."

She changed the topic by saying, "Would it be all right if I took a shower?"

"If you are feeling better, a shower would definitely help."

Even after the shower, Sonia felt no better. Her head ached and her legs felt week. So she once again lay down on the bed and went to sleep. An hour later Kanwal knocked at her door. He wanted to see how she felt and discuss their future program. While talking to her he said, "You still don't look well."

"I'll be all right after I've rested for a while. It's nothing but just a little strain."

"I don't think so. You look all in. Let me check." he said and lifted her face to examine it more closely. "Hmmm...I see."

Sonia had the impression he had diagnosed, for his expression changed. You are right, you need to have complete rest for a day. We should post pone our plans for today and make them for tomorrow."

The authoritative manner in which he had assumed control of the situation unnecessarily annoyed her. She said defiantly, "I know how I feel...I'm not a kid. If I feel like lying down, I'll do it." Saying this she got up from the bed and sat down on the couch, but suddenly felt very weak.

Although she regretted her action, she was adamant because of Kanwal's autocratic manner, for she wanted him to know that he should not take it for granted he had control of her life. But if he had used a little diplomacy, she would have willingly done as he wanted.

A few minutes after Kanwal left, she couldn't sit up any longer, so she slipped between the sheets, glad to be in bed, and admitted that it was really pleasant sometimes to be managed, and regretted having not followed his advise, instead snubbed him.

Sometimes later, Kanwal entered her room without knocking. His approach to bed was almost noiseless. Sonia lay awake, but kept her eyes almost closed. She could feel him looking at her, and fought hard to keep her lids from fluttering, wishing he would stay there. He sat down on the edge of the bed and the touch of his finger tips against her skin was so gentle, she might only have imagined it. "sit up Sonia, and drink this, please." He spoke very softly and held out the cup.

She sat up, took the cup and pulled a face, as she drank.

"You're running a temperature," he said. "The best place for you is the bed. If you think it's okay, I'll draw the curtains to make it cool and dark. A few hours rest will make you feel better."

When Kanwal laid her down on the bed again, his eyes rested briefly on the curves of her breasts pushing against the thin sheet. Then he was gone, leaving her alone in the darkened room with her thoughts.

As he came down stairs, Dr.Henry asked, " How is she now?"

"She is running a temperature and her system is in a state of nervous shock."

"If that's the case she shouldn't travel, because she's not well enough."

"I'll try to dissuade her, if she agrees we could postpone it for a week, but I'm not sure."....and said under his breath.... any more, thinking of her early defiance, and shrugged resignedly. Two hours later he was back in Sonia's bed room with a cup of water and two tablets. He lifted her head to take them. "I want to go to Rome tomorrow as planned," Sonia whispered.

"Not like that, you won't." He insisted and finally he made

her lie down again. "Now close your eyes and go back to sleep. We'll talk this over later."

Kanwal sat down beside her bed, watching to see the effect of his medicine and how soon the fever breaks. His mind too was in a shock, which he had not over come yet, and after a few minutes he too dozed off in his chair.

Two hours later, Sonia opened her eyes. The fever seemed to have finally gone. She saw Kanwal sleeping peacefully. The stubble of three days beard growth darkening the lean jaw. Feeling her hand on him, he woke up.

"Didn't any one ever tell you that chairs weren't made to sleep in." His tawny eyes sparkled at her mutinous expression. He reached out and felt her pulse. "How are you feeling now?"

"You can see, my fever has gone. I feel better. Can I sit up now?"

When he nodded, she sat up in bed. For a moment her vision blurred, but as she shut her eyes the brief dizziness disappeared. Confidently, she got up to go to the washroom.

Next morning right on schedule, they took a taxi to the air-port. It was raining. As the car purred along the freeway, Kanwal put his arm around Sonia and looked sideways at her. "I hope you're well enough to travel."

"Of course, I am." She insisted.

"Do you mind if I check your pulse?"

"Why should I mind?" ventured Sonia.

"I seem to remember, you object to being ....managed." He said hesitatingly.

"I'm sorry, about that Kanwal. Was I....horrid?"

"Very, but I"ll accept your apology."

"As a matter of fact it was rather a relief to be managed."

"Was it, Sonia? should I remember that?"

She looked at him with a complacent expression. "I thought you were enjoying your role as angel of mercy."

"it's my profession that has taught me that," he told her. Then he added, in a very gentle tone, "But you need to relax in the plane, for this journey is going to be a little hard for you after your illness."

"It is nothing really."

By the time they reached the airport, the rain had stopped and the sun was again smiling on the wet streets. As soon as they were air born, Sonia and Kanwal both sat relaxed in their seat

## CHAPTER XIII

After they landed at Rome, Kanwal phoned Neena. George Watson came on the line. He said, "Sir, Neena left for London early morning. She'll be back by tomorrow. I didn't know you were coming. Any way we'll be there very soon."

"Thank you George. We'll be at the lounge."

Paul and George both went to the airport. George wished both Kanwal, and Sonia, picked up their luggage and led them to the car. They were then introduced to Paul. On the way Sonia asked George, "How is Gladys?"

"She is fine, Madam, and she is looking forward to meeting you."

Sonia appreciated Neena's residence and the way she had it decorated. Gladys welcomed them and brought them tea and snacks.

While sipping tea Sonia said, "Where is Narinder?"

"He had a day off. He too has gone. " But she didn't tell

Sonia that they had gone out separately.

An hour later, Kanwal telephoned Dr.Alphonzo, "It's Kanwal. I got here an hour ago."

"I'm really sorry to get the news of your mother. How are you?"

"I'm okay. When can I come to see you."

"I'm free right now."

"I'll be there in an hour."

Before Kanwal left he told Sonia, "You'd better rest. I'm going to meet Dr.Alphonzo. Don't wait lunch for me. I'll be back by the afternoon."

Paul drove Kanwal to the hospital, while Gladys prepared lunch for Sonia. They talked of old times spent together in London. Sonia wanted to ask her about Rajinder, after she left him, but she couldn't find the right words.

At one o'clock Gladys and George retired to their rooms, and Sonia lay down on the couch in the living room and dozed off to sleep. Half an hour later she heard the door bell. She got up and answered it. To her surprise she saw Varinder standing at the door.

For a moment he looked at her before memory dawned. "What are you doing here?" he asked.

"I'm visiting Neena."

"Do you know her?"

"Of course, I know her. And what brings you here?"

"I've come to see my younger brother, Narinder. Is he here?"

"No, he isn't. I don't know when he'll come?"

"Where is Neena?"

"She too has gone out?"

Varinder saw that she was reluctant to let him come in, but he just walked in saying, "I'll wait for Narinder. " After comfortably sitting down on the sofa opposite her he said, "How do you know Neena?"

"She is my daughter, and that's how I know her." The words slipped before she realized what she had done.

"Did you adopt her?" he said with a cynical smile, when he looked at her.

"Why shoud I have adopted her?"

" You know very well that you couldn't have a daughter when your husband was sterile. Perhaps you had a lover." He smirked.

"You are disgusting and I don't want to see your face or talk to you about my personal matters. Leave immediately and only come back when Neena or your brother is here."

"Didn't Neena tell you what I'm planning to do?"

"I don't want to hear anything. Just leave atonce or I'll call George to throw you out."

Varinder got up and said, "Listen carefully. Before I leave here, I want you to know that I'm going to India immediately, to see my son and tell him all about us."

Sonia stared at him, "What do you mean by that?"

"Can you deny that I am the biological father of your son?"

"What proof have you got?"

"I have Dr.Rajinder's diary in which he wrote about artificially inseminating you for a child."

"So what! That doesn't prove anything."

"That's up to the law to understand. Any way, I'm glad I've told you about it. It will now be easy for me to get the custody of my son, in your absence, as you won't be there to oppose it."

Sonia met his cold, challenging stare and knew that this was no idle threat. He meant it. If she didn't do something quickly, he would go to India. The fear of losing her son was enough to blur her rational thinking. In a fit of emotions she said with fists clenched in helpless rage, "Sit down. We need to talk."

His eyes regarded her intently. Then he curiously asked, "What do you want to talk about?"

"How much money can buy me Rajinder's diary, and your promise of not telling Niel anything about it?"

"Do you think your money can buy me?" I just want my son, not your money."

"How about two million pound sterling?"

Varinder hesitated. Two million pound sterling was a comfortable sum to live on. But he thought he could bargain for more. He said,"Don't waste your time?"

"I'm offering you more than what you can ever earn on your own. I'm being generous, because you are my daughter's brother-in-law. Just consider it, or you might lose even this as soon as Narinder comes home." She tried to bluff.

He was a cunning man and he knew she wouldn't have offered her so much money, if she knew her daughter and her husband would back her up. He wanted to try once again from another angle. He stood up as if about to leave and said, "There is one another way, we can solve this problem."

"And what could that be?"

"Just marry me?"

"Are you joking?"

"Why would I joke. I'm quite serious."

There was a lost, frightened look in Sonia's eyes, before she spoke, "Don't you know what our traditions are? How can you even think about it?"

"Talking of traditions, how does artificial insemination go along with it?"

Sonia wanted to say if she knew that she was being

artificially inseminated, she wouldn't have gone for it, but she kept quiet. Not getting any response from her he said, "When your son grows up, and finds out, what would be his reaction?"

Sonia didn't answer. She was thinking of how hard, implacable man he was. She couldn't think rationally. At the moment fear had taken hold of her. She was frightened of his threat of taking away her son from her; so without giving a thought to the consequences she said, "suppose I agree to your proposal.....how...do you...assure me that you won't do anything, to jeopardize my relations with my son?"

"You have to take my word for it. However, when you are my wife, nobody is going to say anything and I'll adopt Niel."

"Let my daughter come home. I'll explain everything to her and then I'll do whatever you say."

"The last plane to India leaves at three. My seat is booked, and I can't postpone my trip." He bluffed, and looked at his wrist watch. "It's now one thirty. We have exactly an hour and a half. Be ready in thirty minutes and we leave."

"What about my seat?" Sonia asked.

"A friend was accompanying me, I'll ask him to take the next flight."

"I'm not packed. How can I leave so suddenly, without....."

Before she could complete her sentence, he said, "If you don't want to be on that plane with me, I'm sorry, I have nothing more to say. Think about it. I need to know exactly what you want to do."

"How about my taking the next plane, after I meet my daughter. I haven't met her yet and I don't want to leave without seeing her. She must be at her work, let me phone her and find out, when she'll be back. If Neena finds out, I have gone off without seeing her, she'll be mad at me."

For a few minutes Varinder stood looking at her. Then suddenly he rushed towards her, and before she was aware, he grabbed her, put a handkerchief in her mouth, and holding her hands at her back, started forcing her towards the stairs. Since Sonia had just recovered from her fever, her vitality being low, she fainted. Seeing her faint, he was scared and he released her hands and took out the cloth from her mouth, and felt her pulse. Finding it all right, he just picked her up and went outside, hailed a taxi and hurriedly got into it.

By chance the taxi driver was Sukhwinder Singh an east Indian. He and his wife had helped Neena move into the house. Seeing Varinder carrying a lady in front of Neena's residence, he was curious and as Varinder had covered Sonia's face, he felt something was fishy, so he wanted to find out who this woman was, but he remained silent, for he didn't want to create any suspicion. He took them to the destination, which was on the outskirts of Rome in a secluded area.

"I guess, the lady is not well. Can I do something?" asked Sukhwinder very politely, as he opened the door for them to get down.

"Thank you, she has these hysterical fits all the time. She'll be all right once she gets her medication." Varinder said and paid him. He then carried Sonia inside, and laid her down on the sofa in the living room. Soon Sonia stirred.

Seeing her come into consciousness, Varinder came forward and stood in front of her, towering over her and looking down into her face with disfavour.

Sonia sat up, and looked around. She was scared and didn't know what to do. She was still thinking, when a frenchman entered the living room. "Hi, Varinder, I didn't expect you so soon. I was going to leave a note for you, as something important has come up, and I have to go out of station for a couple of days. Then looking at Sonia, very pale and shaken, he couldn't resist asking him, "Don't you want to introduce your friend to me?"

"She is Sonia, mother of my son." He said very calmly.

By then Sonia had taken hold of herself and thanked Monsier Phillip specially in french, and told him she needed some help, without his friend knowing about it. He being God fearing and sensible, asked her what it was?

"She spoke in fluent french and asked him to inform Dr.Alphonzo immediately at the General hospital and tell him where to find her. Please refer me to him as Neena's mother."

Varinder looked from one to another as they talked. To keep down his suspicion, Monsieur Phillip spoke in english before he left, "Madam, your french is perfect. When you visit Paris you must come and stay with me."

As soon as Monsieur Phillip was out of the house, Sonia got up and paced the floor ready to explode. She could feel the pressure mounting inside her and the desire to give vent to it was overwhelming. With fists clenching, she stormed at Varinder. "How dare you bring me here? How could you take advantage of my weakness. Once I inform the police, you kidnapped me, you'll be behind the bars for a long time."

Why did you make up this story with a pack of lies. You are definitely not interested in my son. All that you want is money. And I was sincerely offering you a lot of money, but you thought by kidnapping me you would get more. Is that why you kidnapped me?"

"Just calm down. What have I done to make you so angry? I proposed to you and you agreed to marry me. And that's that. " With these words he came closer to her and held her arm, trying to pull her towards him. Sonia tried to pull herself free, but the grip on her arm tightened. Helplessly she said, "By now your friend must have informed my daughter and very soon the police will be here."

Hearing these words Varinder let her go. "You are kidding. My friend would never go against my wishes. If the police comes, I'll tell them you are the mother of my son and since you agreed to marry me, you belong to me. Don't threaten me. And why would I be scared of the police? It would be just your word against mine."

Sonia kept quiet, she wanted to buy some time, so that Kanwal could come to her rescue. She also realized there was no way she could be out of his clutches unless she handled him tactfully. The only way she could stop him from doing anything irrational was to keep him busy talking.

"Look, I agreed to go to India with you because I didn't want my son to know, at this tender age, anything about who his biological father was. I asked you to wait for a while so that I could see my daughter before I left. You took advantage of my fit and brought me here. This really has made me very angry. I promise to go with you if you let me see my daughter and I get my things packed. So why don't you take me back and I ssure you I'll keep my promise."

"How do I know, how sincere you are. Then he came and sat down close to her and said, "Just show me your sincerity by making love to me." With these words he pulled her to him and his mouth found hers with raging insistence, claiming possession as his hands started pressing her body against his own. His move was sudden yet Sonia, inspite of her weak condition, with all her strength, pushed him away and ran towards the terrace. But before she could reach it, he pulled her inside and shut the terrace door tight. Sonia then made a wild plunge to the other door but he caught her. Winding his hand in her hair, he jerked her head back painfully, his eyes dark with unconcealed furry.

When she again tried to pull free, the grip on her hair tightened. She gave a cry of pain, but he didn't loosen his hold on her hair and smirked when he said, "I would rather you come to me willingly, or I'll take you by force, if I have to."

"You can threaten me as much as you like, but I won't do what you want."

She leaned against the wall, her breath coming in frightened little sobs.

"I still intend to take you. I know you don't posses any virtue, still I want to make you an honest woman by marrying you."

By then Sonia had exhausted all her strength. She was a shivering mass of fear. Varinder looked at her, he once again drew her into his arms. The brutality of his embrace left her shaking. There was a look behind his eyes that made her heart jolt sickeningly.

"Please, Varinder, don't do this." She begged.

"Why not?" he answered cruelly. "Why shouldn't you give me what you've probably given to many men to get that daughter of yours. I would have taken you years back if that man, K.K. hadn't saved you."

Sonia's eyes widened in concentration. "How can you say such a terrible lie? You were just trying to scare me then, for you knew you would not only lose your job, you would rot in prison for several years, for my husband would not have spared you at all."

His eyes glittered as he said roughly, now that he is dead, I'm going to take you, and there is no way  other than that."

With these words he picked her up and carried her across the bed. Sonia tried to roll away but he threw himself on her, his full lips hard against her lips. With a fierce hunger of his body, he strove to part her lips with his own. A quivering groan escaped her and she once again collapsed on the bed. Seeing her faint again, he got a little scarred and got up. Then he opened a bottle of whiskey and poured it into a glass, then shook her, "drink this." Since she didn't move , he forcibly put it against her lips and shook her hard. By then she had come around. She tried to push the glass, but he forcibly tried to open her lips and pour the liquid into her mouth. She gulped a little and blasted, "Your behaviour is despicable, get away from me you lousy bastard."Saying this she got out of bed and ran,  but Varinder caught her and once again took her in a tight embrace against a wall. She started hitting his back with her hands; so he pinned them against the wall with his one hand, while his free hand slid under her arms to squeeze her breast.

"What kind of a man are you?" she shouted.

"I've told you, you'd better give yourself to me willingly, otherwise I have no choice but to force myself on you." Then he again carried her to the bed. Sonia was helpless, she had no strength left, and his hand was steadily caressing her breast and there was nothing she could do.

It was nearly two o'clock when Dr.Alphonzo got the message. He told Kanwal about it. "Oh, no. not again." When Kanwal exclaimed, he turned very pale. "Let's rush, she is in danger. We have to be there before he does her any bodily harm."

" Don't worry. I've already informed the police. They'll be there very soon."

Seeing Sonia exhausted and not resisting, Varider was

trying to tear her clothes, when there was a knock at the door and then he heard, "This is police. Open the door."

In another minute the police broke open the door and forcibly dragged him off Sonia. She was partially naked, so thay covered her with a sheet.

"Why are you holding me?" Varinder demanded. "She is the mother of my son. You can ask her."

Sonia had started sobbing in relief. She couldn't speak. And before she could say anything, Kanwal and Dr.Alphonzo arrived.

A few minutes later Sukhwinder, the taxi driver brought George Watson, when he went and told him about how he had taken a lady passenger from Neena's place.

The police insisted that Sonia should give her statement in order to arrest Varinder for attempted rape and abduction. Sukhwinder too gave a statement that Varinder carried the lady unconscious in his taxi.

Sonia was exhausted so Kanwal had no choice but to wrap Sonia in the sheets, she was holding on to and helped her get into the car. She was sobbing.

"Please Sonia, don't cry. He'll never hurt you again."
Later when she was in bed at Neena's place, Kanwal sat on the edge of the bed and said very softly," How did all this happen?"

When he got the whole story he couldn't resist saying, "Why did you at all agree to go with him in the first place, when you knew he could not be trusted."

She was still sobbing. "The fear of losing my son destroyed my rational thinking. At that moment I completely forgot what an uncivilized brute he is."

They were still talking when Neena arrived. She was surprised to see them. Kanwal and Sonia both hugged her and simultaneously asked her where was Narinder."

She replied very coolly, "He is with his friends on a yacht."

"With whom did you go to London?" Was their next question.

Neena looked from one to the other and then said, "I went with Dr. Mohan. I had an important work there." Then she looked at her mother and said anxiously, "Mom, you look very pale. Are you sick?"

"Your mother has been lately sick due to nervous break down. I wanted her to rest in the states before she came here but she was too anxious to come and meet you. there's no need to worry. She'll be okay in a couple of days." Said Kanwal very coolly as if nothing untoward had happened for he didn't want Neena to know the recent attack on her mother by her step brother-in-law. Then looking at Sonia Kanwal said, "No more excitements for the evening. Take this tranqulizer and go to sleep."

Sonia quietly took the tablet and washed it down with a glass of milk.

Kanwal turned off her bedroom lights and within a few minutes Sonia was breathing regularly.


## CHAPTER XIV


Neena followed Kanwal to the living room, and started talking to  him. She first gave her condolence on his mother's death and then asked him anxiously, "I see Mom has a severe nervous breakdown. Please tell me what happened. I know my Mom. I have never seen her like tonight."

"You are right. Something unusual happened today. Then he told Neena everything. Without Dr.Alphonzo's  timely help, I wouldn't have been able to rescue your mother from Varinder. I'm glad everything is over and he can no more hurt her."

There were tears in Neena's eyes, but she held them back. Seeing this Kanwal said, "Look, Neena, your mother had been very brave and holding her head up for such a long time. She really needs some one to look after her. I am worried about her." But before Neena could say something, Kanwal said, "If you had been present here this would never had happened. Although I have no right to ask you, but what was so important that you had to go to London?"

Neena told him all that Varinder had said about his being the biological father, and his intention of taking custody of his son. "Since Narinder was not present, and I was not sure of Mom's programe of coming to Rome, I had to ask Mohan to help me."

"Is he the doctor friend you introduced us at Bombay?"

"Yes."

"What is he doing here?"

"He's got a job here at the hospital where I am working."

"So what did you find out?"

"I'm now quite sure of one thing that Varinder is not the biological father of Niel."

"Are you quite sure."

"I met sister Mary, and she just told me that since the person's semen they had selected, was RH negative, Mom could not be artificially inseminated by it."

"Did she tell you who the donor was?"

"She didn't."

Kanwal heaved a sigh of relief after hearing this. Then he said, "I want you to keep your mother here for a while till she regains her health and self confidence."

"Uncle, do you want me to tell Mom about all that I heard from sister Mary?"

"She is at the moment in a state of nervous exhaustion. Any excitement could have repercussions. You should wait for a few days before you tell her all the facts. She can then talk to sister Mary and find out everything for herself."

They were still talking when George came in and said, "Madam, your husband telephoned to say that he can't come back tonight for there is some engine trouble on the yacht. The party won't be back at Rome for a couple of days."

Hearing this Kanwal said, "We made a mistake of selecting this family for you. Tell me honestly, are you happy in your relationship with your husband?"

"I've tried my best to make this marriage work. I don't think it will last. Narinder married me because of my inheritance and now he knows he can't get what he wanted, his attitude isn't good enough for me. I think if I give him a share of my estate, he'll readily agree for a divorce."

"I know it's your life and you are quite capable of right decisions. Since your mother will be with you, you can do what ever is better for you. I know she'll be a great help in your making a decision. You better go and rest, for its going to be along day, for I understand we have to be at the court for Varinder's hearing."

Kanwal went to his own room. He was very much disturbed. He spent the night tossing and turning in bed. He couldn't decide what he should do. He knew he loved Sonia and he would never try to hurt her feelings.

With the first rays of the sun, he got up, put on his robe and went to the kitchen to prepare tea. Then putting two cups on a tray and some cookies, he knocked at Sonia's door. "Come in the door is open." She said while putting on her robe.

Kanwal came close to the bed, and spoke very softly, "Good morning Sonia. How are you feeling now?"

"I had a restful sleep. I just woke up hearing your knock. You shouldn't have bothered with the tea. Rose Mary would have brought my tea."

"I know, but I wanted to see for myself how you were." Then leaving the tray on the side table Kanwal went to shut the door. Meanwhile the telephone rang. It was Dr. Alphonzo. "Look Kanwal, you don't need to go to the court. I have engaged a lawyer, who'll deal with the case on Sonia's behalf. Let her rest completely."

"Thank you, doctor. I'm so grateful to you."

"Don't thank me. Can I ever forget, how much you did for my daughter, when she was in London? You are a good friend."

"You've already repaid me by looking after Neena and Sonia. I'm really proud to have a friend like you."

After putting down the receiver, Kanwal came close to the bed and handed Sonia a cup of tea. then he filled one for himself and sat on the edge of the bed. He then looked at Sonia and said, "We need to talk."

"I don't get it. what do we need to talk? Is it about my statement to the police. Have we to go there again?"

"All that is taken care of and you needn't bother about it. Just now Dr. Alphonzo told me on the phone."

"Then what do you want to talk about?" When she said this she looked at Kanwal and for the first time noticed, his face was haggard and unshaven, his eyes puffy and red-rimmed from lack of sleep. She had never seen him so distraught.

Kanwal grasped her fingers tightly. His touch sent weakening tremors of yearning through her but she kept her expression calm.

"All that happened yesterday has frightened me. The world is cruel, especially for a woman who is both attractive and rich. I don't want this sort of thing to happen to you ever again. Time and again I have wanted to tell you, but I didn't have the courage. How long can you fight the world single handed? You need a man to look after you and protect you."

Hearing this, Sonia's courage began to falter beneath the forcefulness of his love. He then added very softly, "I want to be with you the rest of my life and look after you. That's all."

Sonia swallowed hard. She didn't want to say what she had to say to him after all that he had done for her. For a second she hesitated, but then taking courage she spoke very coolly, "Kanwal, how can I thank you for all you've done for me. Is that not enough? You know after I came away from London leaving my husband there, I have been taking care of myself very well and most probably I can do it again when I am back in my own country. More over I have no intention of marrying again." She said simply without any emotional outburst. "I've had my chance. You know our traditions and I don't want to break them." Saying these words she tried to pull away her hand from his, but Kanwal didn't let it go.

"Listen, Sonia, we have to be rational. I know the past is something we carry with us always for better or for worse, and Rajinder's memory is something I don't expect you to put aside."

Her throat was constricted, no words came out, and tears were choking her. She was debating within herself. "What happens when he finds out about my past? How can I be able to live with a lie? I know I can't bear to leave him, his companionship, but since he doesn't love me, and wants to sacrifice his other love just out of pity for me, I don't think it's fare. I have to pick up courage and say something which should be reasonable so that we could remain good friends."

"Please, Sonia, take your time and give some thought to my proposal."

"Kanwal, there is nothing to think about. I know quite well that it's best for me to stay single and look after my son." She insisted desperately.

Kanwal turned to look at her, his face white and angry. "Why are you doing this to me?"

"Why can't we remain good friends, for that is the only way I would like to keep." She gulped, trying to withdraw her hand firmly. Please Kanwal, let me go. You didn't bargain for this and I'll not let this happen." She cried, jerking her hand away.

Kanwal once again caught her hand firmly. He wanted to tell Sonia things that were on his mind, but he was not sure what repercussion that would bring. "Don't you trust me? Every thing that I said to you is true. Please use your common sense. I can wait as long as you want me to, but don't decide right now."

Sonia kept quiet. She knew inside her that everything Kanwal had said wasn't true, for she had heard him, with her own ears, promising Ratna on the phone while they were still in Bombay. She therefore couldn't do as Kanwal asked. She was certain he was not in love with her, so she couldn't give in; although she loved him and wanted him with every fibre of her body; and he might have sensed it too, still she couldn't be that selfish. She could sacrifice herself on the altar of love, because she wanted him to be happy. She felt he was willing to sacrifice his life to honour his commitments to his late friend, but she wouldn't let that happen.

Once again Sonia twisted and twirled her hand to free it. Once she freed herself she put her hand on his arm and spoke very softly, "Listen, Kanwal, I know your offer is too good to be turned down, and I have tried to think again and again about it.....though I don't want to hurt your feelings..but I can't...do.. as you suggest."

Kanwal stood up and started pacing the floor. His face was white. Once again he came close to her, put his arm around her, and spoke very gently, "I really want to be with you all my life. I am quite serious, Sonia. Look at me."

But Sonia didn't meet his eyes. How could she agree to his proposal. He never said a word of love being the reason of his proposal. She conjectured that if he was free from his obligations, he would certainly keep his promise to Ratna. It would be better to say goodbye to him now. She therefore concentrated on steadying her breathing. "No," she pleaded, "don't say that. You mustn't say that."

Kanwal gripped her shoulder hard. The fierce determination in his face and the raw pain in his eyes, frightened Sonia. To soothe him, she again said, very tenderly, "Oh! Kanwal! why did you have to spoil our wonderful friendship? I never asked more from you. I never..."

Then she struggled to her feet, in the heat of her emotions forgetting that she had never tied her robe firmly, it slipped down, and her thin nightdress visibly showed all her body contours, before she could pick it up and slide it on. This made her blush. She wanted to rush out of the room as she was determined not to be held by him again as her strength was falling apart. Seeing Kanwal following her, Sonia said, "I've decided to travel around the world for a while and I'm going to look for a female companion. As soon as I find someone suitable, I'll be on my way."

This statement took Kanwal by surprise. He sat down on the couch and said, "I see."  His eyes were a careful mask concealing a depth of pain just below the surface. Then without warning he pulled Sonia into his arms. His kiss was hard and possessive. She stood numb and stunned. Never before had he kissed her so passionately. She jerked away from him, and dragged herself down the stairs with her hands on the rail. She reached the bottom step. "Don't follow me," she said. Her voice was high and tight between gulping breaths. "And don't... say that any more." Then she ran towards the kitchen.

Kanwal stood dumbfounded. He went back to his room and locked himself.

## CHAPTER XV

Late in the morning Neena woke up, and after her morning chore she went to the living room, to find Sonia sitting there.

Meanwhile Gladys laid the table for lunch and came to tell them. In response to that Neena looked at her mother. Sonia said, "I'm not hungry. Why don't you go and have yours?"

"Where is uncle?"   "He must be in his room."

Since Gladys was waiting for them to follow her, Neena said, "I'm not hungry either. You and George have your lunch and retire for the rest of the day. When uncle comes down, I'll serve him."

After a few minutes Sonia went back to her room. Neena sat motionless on the couch, but finally she made up her mind to demand the truth from her mother. Slowly and reluctantly she went and knocked at her mother's door.

"Come in the door is open."

Neena went and sat beside her mother. She looked pale and restless.

"Is something bothering you, Neena? You look so sad?"

"Mom, I know what I'm going to ask you, might hurt your feelings, but I do have a right to ask you."

"I don't understand. You are my daughter, and I have nothing to hide from you."

"Mom, you know Niel was born through artificial insemination. What happened that father was unable to give you this child on his own? Did father at any time become ill after my birth?"

"I don't remember. Why is that important for you to know?"

"Just tell me was he under any sort of treatment for any long term illness?"

"He was quite hale and hearty since I married him. I never saw your father taking any kind of medication."

Neena started pacing the room. She came and stood in front of her mother and hesitatingly said, You know Mom, father was sterile and that is why you were artificially inseminated by another donor and Niel was born." She then knelt down beside Sonia on the rug and taking her hand in hers said very softly with tears in her eyes, "Please mother, tell me, who is my father?"

Abruptly Sonia got to her feet. "What are you talking about?"

"M'm there is no need for you to get excited. I know you've been under lot of stress lately and I don't want you to have another nervous breakdown. I being a doctor, know very well that father couldn't have any child of his own. Then how was I conceived? Just tell me who is my father?" She raised her voice when she asked this.

Sonia's door was not properly closed, and Kanwal had gone down for a glass of water. On his way back he heard Neena's raised voice, asking who was her father. Kanwal's legs suddenly became numb with fright and he stood helplessly outside the door listening.

Sonia knelt beside her dughter on the floor and started crying. "Neena, how can I tell you what happened to me?"

"Please Mom, don't I deserve to know about my father?"

Then between sobs Sonia told her daughter how on her wedding night when she was in the train some one made love to her, and she always thought it was her husband as there was no one else in the coupe which was exclusivly booked for the wedding couple by her father. But when the train stopped, I heard the back door open and shut and then I heard the front door open and your father was saying he had been sitting in the next compartment, for two hours as he had missed the coupe while he went to fill his bottle of water.

"Didn't you tell father what happened in his absence?"

"How could I. I was just sixteen and scared of the person I got married to as I had not even seen him. My father had hastily married me to him because of the deteriorated condition of the country during partition, when rape and abductions were rampant. I was also afraid of my parents, so I kept quiet. When that person jumped from the train, for I heard a thud, I saw a handkerchief on the seat. When I picked it up there was a photograph of a young boy in it."

"Do you still have that photograph?"

"Yes, I've always kept it."   "Can I see it?"

Sonia took out the handkerchief and the photograph, and gave it to Neena. Seeing the photo for a moment she looked shocked, then very softly she asked, "Don't you know who he is?"

"I have no idea. Do you know him?"

"Yes, I think so." She stopped abruptly. She clearly remembered one day when she had gone  to Kanwal's house, and her mother had pointed at the photo in the album she was looking, " Look at my son when he was young. He looked exactly like you."

Neena remembered asking her when the photo was done and she told her when he was in the tenth grade."

Sonia once again asked Neena, "Do you really know him?"

"I have a vague idea of seeing such a photo some where. But you need not worry I know I'll soon remember where I saw the photo."

Hearing these words Kanwal rushed to his room and locked his door. He was now quite certain of the past he always dredded. He now knew he had no choice but leave immediately before Neena comes and questions him. He packed his bag and stepped out of the house and went off.

For a while Neena stayed with her mother trying to bring her around. She went to the kitchen and brought two cups of tea and both sat down drinking silently. She then gave her mother a tranquilizer.

She quietly left the room after Sonia went to sleep. She then knocked at Kanwal's door but getting no response and thinking him to be resting she went to her room and decided to see him later.

In the evening, she wanted to talk to Kanwal and when she came there, she once again knocked. There was no reply. She tried the handle and found it open. She enterd the room. There was no one there. The room was empty. All the clothes were gone. Then her eyes was caught by an envelope lying on the table. She picked it up. It was addressed to Sonia.

Neena then went to her mother's room and seeing her awake, said, "I think uncle has left. I saw this envelope on the table. It is addressed to you. You'd better get up and read it."

Sonia's heart beat fast. With trembling hands she opened the envelope and began to read, but tears kept blinding her. Seeing this Neena said, "Do you mind if I read it to you?"

Sonia handed her the letter. Neena sat down beside her mother and started reading.

Dear Sonia:

I don't know how to put into words all that I want to tell you, after all that we both went through in these couple of months. I know what I'm going to disclose will not only shock you but you wouldn't like even to see my face or have anything to do with me. Today when I was coming up from the kitchen I heard Neena's raised voice imploring you to tell her who was her father. I was genuinely shocked and stood beside your door to listen, not out of curiosity but I needed some sort of confirmation to my doubts that had been gnawing me from the time of Neena's wedding.

I've brought nothing but misery and unhapiness in your life. I had no idea that I had left a photo behind when I jumped out of the train after my henious act, when I destroyed your virginity by raping you in the train on your wedding night.

When I saw your wedding saree, the night before Neena's wedding, and I commented I had seen one like that before, You told me that this saree was one of a kind which was made exclusively for you by the weaver, your father's friend. I was shocked but I couldn't voice my doubt although all the circumstances proved it could be me only, for I knew by staying with you all these months that you were not the kind of person to have any affair before or after your marriage, although I had these doubts when Rajinder told me he was sterile.

I have never told any one how all this happened to me.

Today when Neena told you that she had recognized the photo, it's time I should tell my story before my daughter comes and questions me.

I was a spoilt child of rich parents. I had bad company and very early in life had started drinking and gambling. The day you boarded the train at Amritsar I had taken a few drinks too many and as the train started I jumped into the first compartment I could hold on and unluckily it was your coupe. I saw you sitting with your face covered in a beautiful saree and when I sat close to you, there was no objection from you. When I tried to touch you you didn't object. I now realize you must have thought it was your husband. Before the train entered the next station I jumped out of the train from the back door, and I didn't see another train coming from the  opposite direction. I would have been crushed to death but a young saint came from nowhere and rescued me.

Under his Lotus feet I learnt the meaning of life and gained lot of wisdom. I wanted to stay there all my life just to punish myself but Sai Ram wanted me to go out into the world to help the down trodden. I went to my parents, studied hard, passed my pre-medical and then went to England for further studies.I vowed to remain a celibate just to punish myself for this immoral act.

Since then there has been no woman in my life. I don't know how and when I fell in love with you. The first time we met in the club library room I was certainly attracted to you. You looked lovely and I thought you were different. Next day when I went purposely to the club, hoping to meet you, I couldn't find you. I never forgot your lovely face. Then suddenly I saw you again at the hospital Golden Jubilee party. I must have fallen in love with you then when you danced with me and I held you trembling in my arms. I was not aware that you were Dr.Rajinder's wife, for you told me in certain words that you were single.

One day I told Dr.Rajinder how I raped a bride who had a mole under her right breast, but I never saw her face. I now recollect how pale he turned hearing this. It was only then that he decided to come to India to question you, to learn the truth.

I was really stunned to see you in Delhi as Rajinder's widow. Later I wanted to woo you and get married to you, but accidently I came across your wedding saree and so I had to control my feelings till such time I was sure you too loved me. I didn't want to hurt you again and although I loved you, I was scared that if you knew the facts, you would hate me and never allow me to be near you.

Then came the revelation that Niel too was my son when you told me that he had a birth mark just like me. I left for London to find out the truth. sister Mary confirmed it. The day you were artificially inseminated, I had just got my medical done. Sister Mary came to me and asked me to give my sperms for artificial insemination for a patient immediately. When I enquired what was the emergency, she told me the semen they had selected was from a person whose RH was negative and it was not possible to use that. Just to oblige sister Marry with whom I had very good relations during my internship I agreed. Even then I went to India to get my paternity checked and I found Niel to be my son. I wished to tell you all about it when I came back from India, but I was scared as to how you'll take the news as on no account I wanted to lose you being madly in love with you. Today after you rejected me down right, I think I have totally failed and perhaps that is the punishment I really deserve.

I now feel my life is over. I do regret that I couldn't have a chance to tell my two children, I am their father and perhaps you too should not disclose this fact for I don't think I deserve it. I have now decided to go back to the Sai Ashram and stay there for the rest of my life.

I've already made my new Will. All my assets in England, which amount to approximately fifty million pound sterling, go to you. Out of my estate in India fifty million will go to Karan and the rest, which consists of thirteen villages, numerous houses and high rise buildings, shares, securities, etc amounting to two billion rupees, is for Niel. I've also put five million pound sterling in Neena's account at Rome for her.

Goodbye, and the best of luck in your travels. Please don't try to hate me.


Kanwal.


By the time Neena finished reading the letter, tears were streaming down both their cheeks. Sonia fainted. Neena brought her around and laid her on the couch. She then knelt beside her mother and said, "Mom, now what?"

"I don't know what to say. You know sometimes I felt I've met him somewhere whenever he was close to me, but I couldn't recollect. Do you think I should hate him?"

"It's not for me to judge. Tell me did uncle propose to you today?"

"Yes, he did. I thought if I rejected him he would marry Ratna, whom he loved, but I was wrong. Perhaps he kept this charade just to keep me from disclosing my feelings for him."

"Tell me, do you love him?" Neena asked hesitatingly.

Sonia just nodded. Her throat was too tight for words. "Would you like to follow him?"

"What do you think I should do?"

"Just tell me what you want. I know he made a mistake in his life and have suffered a lot. If you really love him and can forgive him, this is the time for you to go after him before he enters the Ashram. I can arrange for your passage to India just now for I know some one who can do it."

"Try if you can."

Neena called her friend who told her that the last plane to India was due at six in the evening and she could collect the ticket for her mother at the airport. Neena summoned Paul and asked him, "Can you get us to the airport in time to catch the six o'clock plane?"

"Yes, Madam."

Sonia was the last to board the plane. As soon as she settled down, the plane became airborne.

Once they were out of their seat belts, Sonia went around the plane looking for Kanwal. He wasn't there. She then asked the air hostess, "Will you please check if there's a gentleman named Dr.Khanna in the first class compartment?"

In a few minutes the young woman came back and said, "Yes, Madam, he is aboard."

Sonia with a little hesitation entered the first class compartment. She saw Kanwal reading a newspaper. She came and stood beside him. Kanwal saw her and was stunned. He couldn't believe his eyes. He stood up but made no attempt to speak or touch her.

Seeing the lady stand, the man seated beside Kanwal said, "I'm going to see a friend in the other cabin. If you like you can just use my seat."

Sonia sat down. She didn't have the courage to speak. She didn't know what to say. Seeing her in this plight, Kanwal said, "I'm really sorry Sonia. I know you are very angry and if you want I can submit myself to the police for the crime I had committed. I'm prepared for that too if that can help you get over the pain and sufferings I have been instrumental about."

Hearing this Sonia had to say something. She spoke very softly, "You always told me to forget the past, and that's what I'm going to do right now. Perhaps that was destined and I know you too have suffered its consequences. I am at least relieved that my children have a father. This fact was killing me all the time. I was always puzzled as to why you never got married. I tried several times to find out from your mother but she didn't have any clue, so she said. I also wanted to ask you myself, but some how my courage failed. Tell me, why you made a sudden decision of giving Neena in marriage as your daughter? Were you quite sure about you being her father or just because of not having Rajinder present at the wedding as you said earlier?"

"Why do you want to know? Can that help you or the children?"

"I'm just curious."

"Please don't side step the issue. Tell me why are you going to India? Do you think I'm a threat to Niel?"

"Please Kanwal don't say all these things. Such a sarcasm is not good for your health. Do you think I am that kind of a person? Do you really want to know why I am here?"

"I do." He said and a smile flickered on his lips.

Sonia saw this and she held Kanwal's hand and said, "I know how you feel about me. I was blind not to see your love. I was under the impression that you were obliging me, to compromise Rajinder's death. Why I didn't accept your proposal, because I thought you wanted to marry Ratna but at the same time you were obliged to me."

Hearing this Kanwal put his arm around Sonia and said very tenderly, "Have you pardoned me?"

Sonia saw tears glistening in his eyes. She put her hand on his before she said, "I'm sorry Kanwal for giving you so much pain."

For the next hour they both sat silently with hands joined. Then Kanwal arranged through the air hostess for Sonia to fly first class the rest of the flight.

After they settled down, Kanwal put his finger under her chin, tilted up her face and said, "Look into my eyes. What do you see there?"

But Sonia closed her eyes. She didn't have the courage to see the pain in his eyes. She knew he was repenting for what happened to them two decades back. She just came closer to him and held his hands.

When the plane landed at Heathrow Airport, Kanwal said, "We are getting down here."

Aren't we going to India?" Sonia questioned.

"How do I know when you reach India you won't change your mind and run away from me?" he said lightly. "I can't afford to lose you. let's get married, and then we'll go to India for our honeymoon."

"What about my mother? How will she take it?"

"Don't worry. When I was in India, I told your mother about getting married to you. I also told her about Niel being my son. She gave her blessings."

"You never told me."

"I was too scared."

Having cancelled the rest of the flight, Kanwal took her to

his bachelor apartment. Arther Newbury was surprised to see them. Kanwal introduced Sonia as his fiancee. Arthur shook hands with her and asked, "How do you do, Madam?"

Later Kanwal dialed his friend Dr.Hardy. "Doctor, it's Kanwal."

"When did you get in?"

"An hour ago. Hardy, can you do something for me?"

"Sure, what is it?"

"I want to get married today. Can you arrange a time with the registry office?"

"Sure. It's a piece of cake. Mr.Brown is my friend. I don't think he'll turn down my request. I'll let you know in half an hour."

Kanwal went back to where Sonia was sitting. She poured tea that Arthur had brought in. Both sat down and sipped the tea quietly.

As soon as the telephone rang, Kanwal grabbed the receiver.

From the other end Dr.Hardy spoke, "You must be in the office by one o'clock. I'll be there. Congratulations."

"Thank you. You have solved my dilemma."

Kanwal looked at his watch. It was noon. He sat down beside Sonia. "Look, we are going to be married today at one o'clock. Would you like to freshen up or change?"

He then took her to his bedroom and closed the door behind them, and drew her gently into his arms. His breath was soft and warm against the sensitive areas of her skin. before he kissed her he said, "If you still have any regrets, please Sonia there is plenty of time to think it over." In stead of replying Sonia put her arms around his neck and stood on her toes to make her face come closer to his. Kanwal did not lose a second and kissed her passionately on the lips and then all over her face and her neck as though she were a gift too precious for words.

"Won't we be late if you don't let me change? Are you not going to freshen up and shave?" Sonia said impishly. He laughed and left her.

Dr.Hardy met them outside the registry office. He had a bouquet in his hand. Kanawal introduced Sonia to him. The doctor shook hands with her and then presented her with the flowers. On the way to the office Kanwal selected a ring with a solitaire diamond.

After they both signed the register Kanwal put the ring on Sonia's finger. The magistrate congratulated them. Dr.Hardy and Kanwal's lawyer Mr. Michael English, witnessed the marriage certificate. Later Dr.Hardy threw a party in their honour at Hotel Skyline, on Bath road near the Airport.

## CHAPTER XVI

At Gulmarg in Kashmir, Sonia and Kanwal checked into Sheraton Hotel. It was six in the evening, and the snow on the mountains around them glistened under the stars. Sonia was shy as any teenage bride.

Kanwal came close and his arms tightened around her waist while his lips brushed her hair. Joy surged through her in slow pulsating waves. "Darling, how I've longed for this moment. You'll never know how close I often came to grabbing you."

Sonia didn't answer, just laid her head on his chest. She started visulising how he had grabbed her the first time in the train, and she thought her husband was rather mad doing it that way.

"You look sad. Am I over doing it?"

Sonia looked up and their eyes met. Suddenly Kanwals thoughts too mingled with hers on the night in the train. For a second he hesitated amd it showed all over his face. Then with a cool and composed face he said, " Sonia, earlier you asked me when I first fell in love with you. Do you want to hear it?"

"Does it matter anymore?"

"But I want to tell you."

"I'm listening."

"I  fell in love with you the first time I touched you. You know I never forgot that sensation I had then and to keep your memory alive I named my house at Bombay, THE BRIDE. I also got a statue ordered with a big black mole under your right breast." While saying this Kanwal lifted her blouse and started carassing the mole as he had done two decades back.

Sonia kept quiet. How could she tell him that after that event she never liked her husband making love to her. She too never had the same sensation again till tonight. Then the moon arose in the sky and gradually its light flooded the room. Kanwal picked up Sonia and laid her on the bed and slowly and skillfully removed all her clothes except her slip. Then he too lay close to her in an embrace. He could see the pale lavender slip with its wide lace edging forming delicate shadows against her breasts and thighs in the moonlight. Slowly he slipped down the straps, then drew the garment over her hips and discarded it. They were now lying together, flesh against flesh, his naked limbs entwined around hers just as she had yearned for so often.

The warmth of their bodies glowed to fire. His hand cupped the roundness of her shoulders and trailed gently down to the curves of her hips. His mouth sought the softness of her breasts. She wound her fingers in his brown curling hair with a little moan as his tongue sent shivers of electricity on fine wires from the sensitive tips of her nipples to the core of her abdomen.

He followed the path with his mouth, placing gentle kisses along her ribs, and when his lips came to that beautiful mole he had earlier touched, he once again caressed it with maddening deliberation before going on to explore the naval.

Sonia's hand moved restlessly over his body, tracing the strong cords of his neck, the muscles of his back. Then they slid down to feel the hardness of his buttocks. His strong thighs gently seperated hers as he went into her lightly, his hands cupping her face.

Their union was easy and natural because they were both in perfect harmony. After all she knew what it was to make love to him. She felt the same exhilaration she had felt twenty four years ago, despite her shock and fear. She was transported beyond the sensual experience into realms where minds and spirits as well as bodies were in perfect unisons.

When the peaks of star-bursting joy had faded into the shimmery stillness of the night, they lay wrapped in each other's arms, contented, unwilling to move apart even a few inches or for that matter, for a single moment.

At length Kanwal stirred to bring his lips to her neck, his breath warm and gentle on the curves of her jaw. He kissed her throat, her ear, her hairline. "O, Sonia, darling, Queen of my heart!" He murmured huskily, his arms once again tightening around her as his head lay against her breasts. "I have to make up for all these years of wanting it this way."

Sonia smoothed his hair. "Now we have a lifetime together." She said softly, her voice husky with contentment.

"O! my precious one: How I love you and want to worship you on a pedestal."

"I love you too, my darling." with these words her lips met his in a flood of contentment and happiness too great to be expressed in words. Now her back was turned on the past, and her arms held a future filled with a promise of a lifetime.

**********************************